The Dark Figure: Crime in Victorian Bolton

By David Holding

First published by
Scott Martin Productions, 2019
www.scottmartinproductions.com

Published in Great Britain in 2019 by
Scott Martin Productions
10 Chester Place,
Adlington, Chorley, PR6 9RP
scottmartinproductions@gmail.com
www.scottmartinproductions.com

Electronic version and paperback versions available for purchase on Amazon.
Copyright (c) David Holding and Scott Martin Productions.

First edition 2017.

All rights reserved. Without limiting the rights under copyright reserved above, no part of this publication may be reproduced, stored or introduced into a retrieval system, or transmitted, in any form or by any means (electronic, mechanical, photocopying, recording or otherwise), without the prior written permission of both the copyright owner and the publisher of this book. No paragraph of this publication may be reproduced, copied or transmitted save with written permission or in accordance with the provisions of the Copyright Act 1956 (as amended).

Front cover photograph provided to the author by the Local Studies Department in Bolton Central Reference Library for the author's MA dissertation. Stylistic editorial amendments made.

Acknowledgements

It is always difficult to remember when undertaking research of any kind, all the people who helped along the way with advice, encouragement and information. I wish to express my thanks to those who played a pivotal role in bringing this work from its initial conception to full fruition. My thanks also go to those anonymous yet ever helpful staff at the numerous institutions I have consulted. I would like to express special thanks and appreciation to the following:

Lancashire County Record Office, Preston.
Bolton Central Reference Library and Local Studies Department.
The Manchester Metropolitan University Local Studies Department.
The Staff at the Greater Manchester Police Museum, Newton Street, Manchester.

Acknowledgement is also paid to my fellow social historians, and members of the legal profession and magistracy, for the benefit of their expertise on the various issues raised in this work. My gratitude loses no sincerity in its generality. I would hasten to add, that none of the above are responsible for the contents of this work, any mistakes are entirely my own.

David Holding, 2019

David Holding

Introduction

Studies focussing on crime in Britain during the nineteenth century have tended to concentrate on the country at large with a particular emphasis on the London area.[1] There are obvious advantages in taking this approach; for one thing, it allows researchers to draw upon a wide range of printed and manuscript material. The temptation to concentrate on London is also strong as its problems were given extensive coverage before Select Committees, Royal Commissions and with parliamentary debates, as well as being covered by newspapers, journals and literature of the period.

Historians' neglect of crime in relatively small towns in favour of the large cities has tended to oversimplify the perceptions of crime in Britain during the nineteenth century. Yet for most historians, individual cities and towns constitute the most attractive scale of analysis for understanding crime and criminality. There are many compelling reasons for following this route, both in terms of the concerns and methodologies of social history and the realities of Victorian society. The town constitutes a convenient point of analysis for marshalling and manipulating the data available in police and court records which have done much to deepen and inform our understanding of crime in nineteenth century Britain.

In one sense it is fitting that one rapidly developing industrial town in Lancashire should be taken as the focus for analysing the nature and extent of criminal activity during the nineteenth century. This study of Bolton covers the period from 1850 to 1880. It adopts a pragmatic approach to crime by focusing primarily on street offences, property crime, violence against the person, vagrancy, vice and drink-related offences, including breaches of the peace. Excluded from the equation are political crimes and offences arising from industrial disputes leading to civil disorder. These bear little relationship to everyday crime and have been highlighted in other substantial works.

This study is a traditional historical one based on documentary survey and analysis of court and police records, to assess changes over time and to relate such changes to their economic, social and political contexts. The primary quantitative

---

[1] J.A. Sharpe, *Crime in Early Modern England, 1550-1750*, Longman, London 1984.

source used in the study was the Bolton Borough Police Chief Constables' Annual Reports to the Watch Committee covering the period from 1850 to 1880. Qualitative sources include government papers, official reports and town records, together with the selective use of local newspaper reports.

The study is organised in the following way. The first chapter focuses upon the formation of the Bolton Borough Police Force, its administration and effectiveness as a peace-keeping body. Chapter two examines those institutions providing outlets for criminal activity in Victorian Bolton. Chapter three focuses on the methodological and substantive issues relating to crime in Bolton - the 'statistical' overview. The use of statistical date for historical research is now a common practice. It is advantageous because many of the processes and methods have been tested in previous works and are well-documented.[2] However, the methodological techniques employed in this analysis of crime data are innovative in that they have not previously been applied to a study of crime in Bolton. Chapter four considers the various forms of sentencing, and the use and value of punishments, and questions their ultimate effectiveness.

This study addresses four key questions; in what way was crime a reflection of the social and economic life of Bolton during the period? What sort of institutions or habits acted as stimulants to crime in its various forms? What patterns or trends emerge from the statistical data and how reliable are they? How did the police, the courts and reformative bodies react to the flood of crime, and how effective were they? A definition of crime which satisfies every generalisation is probably impossible. The simplest definition describes crime as behaviour which violates the criminal law. There are, however, problems with this definition.

Some public order legislation gives citizens and law officers, particularly police officers, discretionary powers which can be used if considered necessary. Among the most obvious examples are threatening, abusive or insulting words or behaviour with intent to provoke a breach of the peace and, of course, resisting or obstructing a constable in the execution of their duty. This kind of discretionary power increased with the growth of the new police during the nineteenth century.

---

[2] E.A. Wrigley (ed) *Nineteenth century society: Essays in the use of quantitative methods for the study of social data*, Cambridge University Press, 1972.

Most people would differentiate between these offences and what they consider to be 'real' crime such as murder, rape and theft with violence. Nevertheless, the definition of crime as behaviour violating the criminal law has the advantage for the historian of relating behaviour to laws in force at a particular time; thus 'criminal' behaviour is tied very firmly to its historical context. It is this definition which informs this study.

Intra-communal disorders consisting largely of drunken brawls, quarrels between neighbours and domestic disputes were a regular feature of most working-class districts of towns throughout the nineteenth century. This type of violence was not of particular interest to the police or magistrates unless it spilled over into the public domain. There is no doubt that attempts by provincial police forces after 1856 to monitor working-class districts more closely, made those living on the periphery of crime particularly vulnerable to police surveillance.

Bolton, as with other Lancashire towns in the nineteenth century, experienced the social problems and contrasts of wealth and poverty, prosperity and depression. The late 1830s and 1840s were the years of the most acute anxiety, which fed on economic depression as well as the radical and industrial agitation culminating in 1842. During the period covered by the study, it was the small opportunist crime which was statistically the most common in Bolton. The more 'public' offences of prostitution, drunkenness, breaches of the peace and vagrancy all featured prominently in local crime statistics.

The statistical patterns of crime appear to follow concerns about social order, though the coincidence between the troughs of the business cycle and the peak of crime would suggest that there were some links between economic necessity and petty theft. The debate on the standard of living of the early nineteenth century working-class is a historical controversy that has continued without abatement. However, whether or not the overall standard of living declined or improved, there is little question that there were periods of severe hardship and distress for large numbers of Bolton's working class. Crime was just one manifestation of this distress.

Those particular districts of Bolton with high concentrations of working-class residents were expected to be the hot-beds of crime and disorder. The anti-social behaviour of some working-class people as reflected in the 'imperfect' crime statistics, merely reinforced preconceived notions regarding the working-class and crime. It will be argued that crime in Bolton cannot be satisfactorily addressed if isolated from the wider societal developments taking place in the town throughout the nineteenth century.

Chapter One:

Development of the Bolton Borough Police

From as early as 1190, Bolton in common with all parishes in the country had Justices of the Peace as the chief law enforcement agency. These Justices were appointed by the Crown and were elected from amongst the notable members of the parish. Initially, their duties were restricted to the appointment and supervision of the parish constables. It was only later that Justices were empowered to try offenders and punish them. There were few safeguards to ensure that suitable people were appointed to the position of Justice and consequently many unscrupulous men were selected.

In Bolton, the appointment of the parish constables was made for a period of twelve months. The position was unpaid, and the duties were wide and varied. They included 'the inspection and maintenance of roads, bridle-paths and bridges, the collection of rates, the apprehension and detention of law breakers and, on occasions, their punishment'.[3] It became the practice for the selected person to accept the position and then pay someone to undertake the duties. The idea was to find someone who would do the job for the least pay. Inevitably, this resulted in the persons engaged being virtually unemployable for any other work. However, these early forms of 'policing' were essentially local in origin.

To assist the constable, the Justice would appoint one or two deputies known as 'watchmen' who were paid very little. From 1812 to 1820, Bolton had a 'Watch and Ward', which was a purely voluntary body for the purpose of maintaining and securing a vigilant supervision of the town. The 'Watch and Ward' Rules were that 'two conductors were to be appointed for every night's watch, each to conduct ten men; one half to remain in the 'Watch' room during the time the others were on duty unless in case of emergency'.[4]

The Watch was to remain on duty from 10.00 p.m. until 6.00 a.m. In addition, eight Ward men were to be on duty each day from 6.00 a.m. to 1.00 p.m. and four from 1.00 p.m. to 10.00 p.m. The duties of the members were not onerous; they had to

---

[3] R.J. Goslin, *'Duty Bound': A History of Bolton Borough Police,* (Bolton, 1970), p.14.
[4] J.C. Scholes, *History of Bolton,* p. 471.

report and deal with incidents of drunkenness, mainly attributed to the all-night sittings at a number of town centre public houses. They do not appear to have had much success in their attempts as this entry in the Minute Book records:

> 'We have endeavoured to attend to our duty, particularly in search of public houses where we heard quarrelsome conduct. We are told we had no business in these houses; if that is the case, we consider the main purpose of the Watch and Ward is rendered fruitless'.[5]

The great problem of English police work has long been the difficulty of reconciling effective police action with individual freedom. Prior to the Industrial Revolution, an uneasy compromise existed between Justices and parish constables in managing the 'Watch and Ward' of each small township. The demographic explosion and the onset of large-scale urbanisation deprived the townships of this ancient advantage, and criminal disorder pressed hard on the outmoded and ill-equipped authorities.

---

[5] *Bolton Watch and Ward Minute Book: Entry for 7th January 1820*, (Bolton Archives Department).

Police Reform

There already existed some tradition of police reform before the nineteenth century. After the Gordon Riots, the novelist Henry Fielding had initiated some magisterial reform under the Middlesex Justices Act of 1792, which introduced magistracy and the grouping of constables. The Manchester Justices first implemented these ideas in 1795, followed by the Lancaster Justices in 1805. A strong school of thought believed that private enterprise was by far the soundest approach, with common informers, insurance companies and thief-takers being regarded as major weapons in the fight against crime.

The great propagandist for a professional preventive police force was Edwin Chadwick, a leading member of the Benthamite circle, and a man who had made police reform one of his several special subjects. One of the most lucid and most publicised expositions of Chadwick's viewpoint was the Constabulary Report of 1839. Its official title was the "First Report of the Commission Appointed to Inquire as to the Best Means of Establishing an Efficient Constabulary Force in the Counties of England and Wales".

Three principal steps are discernible in Chadwick's argument; the poor state of law enforcement, especially in view of the radical social changes, rendered the criminal life a possibly prosperous one. Chadwick having observed that crime thwarted the policy of 'laissez-faire', a scheme of action was required. A large and well-organised body of men could render the infraction of personal and property rights a difficult task. A typically rational attitude was developed towards the organisation of the police.

The Commission urged the abandonment of 'management by a body of uniformed and virtually irresponsible persons'. Chadwick had always wanted the police to be a centralised 'national' establishment. The Metropolitan Police suggested the Report could act as the focus for 'central control with local management'. When firm plans were mooted, the objections came from all expected quarters. Many Tories and some Whigs were fearful of state encroachment and the popular press stirred up a fiery opposition. Another important factor in the need for reform was the danger of mob action for social and political reasons. In the new crowded urban areas, working-class unrest was apparent before Chartism became prominent. During the St. Helens coal strike of 1831, special constables proved to be ineffective, and the 10th Hussars had to be sent for to maintain order.

Historians of the period have noted 'the remarkable synchronisation of these outbreaks', although it is accepted that 'spontaneous tumult' in various places was the real danger. However, by the beginning of 1840, the 'tumultuous upheaval' had subsided. Certainly, the threat of mass action was a frightening one to the middle and upper classes in the area, although Read notes how rapidly the Chartist position had declined by 1839.[6]

In 1832, the Reform Bill became law and as a result Bolton became enfranchised. The old Court Leet was replaced by a Town Council of elected representatives. Bolton was incorporated as a Borough under the provisions of the Municipal Corporations Act of 1835, by which the town could be granted a Charter of Incorporation. Under this Charter, government of the town would be by an elected Town Council with powers to form and maintain a police force. Quite naturally, there were vested interests in maintaining the status quo of local government in Bolton, and this gave rise to fierce opposition to the proposals for incorporation. Most of this opposition came from the Conservatives who maintained that the existing system of local government, Courts Leet, Borough Reeves and constables was quite efficient for the needs of the town.

Representations both for and against the change in local government were made to Parliament. However, the Charter of Incorporation was provisionally granted on the 11th October 1838. One important effect of the Charter that covered the townships of Great and Little Bolton and the Haulgh, was to introduce six electoral Wards, entitled to have representatives on the Town Council. These Wards were to be known as Exchange, Bradford, Derby, Church, East and West. Despite the provisional granting of the Charter, the Conservatives refused to accept it and questioned its legality. When an election was organised for the appointment of town councillors, the Conservatives refused even to offer a candidate for election. Notwithstanding, an election went ahead, and a Town Council was formed, the first meeting being held on December 1st 1838, and a Watch Committee being formed on December 20th.

One of the first acts of the Watch Committee was to introduce a police force but, because of the continued opposition

---

[6] D. Read, 'Chartism in Manchester' in A. Briggs (ed), *Chartist Studies* (1965), pp. 29-50.

to the acceptance of incorporation, there were grave doubts as to the legality of such a force. Unfortunately records of this period are disjointed and incomplete.[7] Eventually twelve men were appointed to make up a new police force in Bolton, and this became operational on the 18th February 1839 under the Rural Constabulary Bill of that year, and lasted more or less on a full-time basis until November of that year. This first Bolton force comprised one superintendent, one inspector and ten constables. It is a remarkable fact that in 1839, two separate police forces were in operation in the town; constables under the control of the Trustees of Great and Little Bolton, and the Corporation's 'new' police. This gave rise to frequent conflict and confusion, and antagonism was rife between the two forces. To make matter even more complex, inquests in the town had to be conducted twice, resulting in a chaotic situation.

---

[7] Goslin, *'Duty Bound'*, p. 18.

Recruitment and Administration

On November 5th 1839, Sir Charles Shaw, Commissioner of the Manchester Police Force, swore in the first forty men. The Bolton Police Act of August 1839 created the power to form a police force, yet this first body was in effect, a Government Force although control was delegated to the Town Council. It was only in 1842 with a further Act of Parliament, that control was effectively given to Bolton Corporation. On September 7th 1842, overall control of the police was given to the Town Council and delegated to the Watch Committee. The decision (for whatever reason) was also taken to reduce the force from forty to twenty police officers. In 1842, the Bolton Force was distributed as follows:

Great Bolton	2 PCs [Day]
Great Bolton	2 PCs [Night]
Little Bolton	1 PC [Day]
Little Bolton	1 PC [Night]
Church Ward	2 PCs
Bradford Ward	2 PCs
Exchange Ward	2 PCs
Derby Ward	2 PCs
East Ward	2 PCs
West Ward	2 PCs
Patrol	1 Inspector, 1 Sergeant

Although it is possible by looking at records to obtain limited information on the first forty people to join the Bolton force, it would certainly be revealing to understand the motive that prompted them to join. Emsley has suggested some possible reasons; 'The uniformed police constable received a modicum of training, much of it military-style drill, before being put on his beat. Few of the early recruits seem to have conceived of the police as a career; many appear to have volunteered to tide them over a period of unemployment'.[8] Certainly, the remuneration received by the early Bolton police was such that would not encourage long service. A superintendent received £120 per annum, whilst an inspector was paid £1. 16s 11d per week, a sergeant received £1 5s per week and constables 17s per week.

---

[8] C. Emsley, *Crime and Society*, p. 191.

When these figures are compared to the weekly average wage in Bolton it can be seen that the starting wage in the police was well below average:

Male Cotton Spinner	-	£1. 15s. 0d.
Male Coal Miner	-	£1. 8s. 6d.
Male Brass Founder	-	£1. 2s. 0d.
Male Labourer	-	10s. 0d.[9]

Another aspect of early police service was the restrictions on the constable's ability to make additional money 'outside the job':

'Unlike the wife of a rural worker, the country policeman's wife was forbidden to keep a cow and the urban policeman's wife could not run a small shop'.[10]

The payment of wages to police officers appears to have been a chancy affair. Each month's pay lists submitted to the Watch Committee by the superintendent would be subjected to careful scrutiny before payment was authorised. With the exception of age and height requirements (under thirty-five years and over five feet six inches), there does not appear to have been any other qualification for appointment to the Bolton force. According to Goslin, the majority of the original entrants 'were incapable of reading or writing, but as paper work then attached to law enforcement was minimal, this deficiency was not a great drawback'.[11]

---

[9] J. Ginswick, *Labour and the Poor in England and Wales*, (1983), Appendix 2.
[10] J. Ginswick, 'Life on a Labourer's Wage', *Police Review*, March 1983, pp. 651-2.
[11] Goslin, *'Duty Bound'*, p.22.

1839	Drunk on Duty.	21
	Attempting to extract liquor from Barmaid.	2
1840	Offences involving Drink.	20
	Neglect of Duty.	3
	Absent from Beat.	2
	Unfit through Health.	1
	Appropriating money from Prisoner.	1
	Absent from Duty all Night.	1
1841	Exposing Person to Prostitute.	2
	Convicted Felon.	1
	Assault with Intent to commit Rape.	1
	Striking man with Truncheon.	2
	Insolence to Superior Officer.	1
1842	Making False Statement.	1
	Using unbecoming Language.	1
	Being in Plain Clothes whilst on Duty.	1
	Unsatisfactory Character.	1
	Offences involving Drink.	15
	Inefficiency.	3
	Boasting of having interfered with a married woman	1
	Taking Indecent liberties with two females whilst on Duty.	1
	Stealing from Police Office.	1

[12]

The first forty men joining the Bolton force appear to have been a mixed bag of working-class persons, varying from totally incompetent to consistent in the discharge of their duties. Those men who fell from grace and were subsequently dismissed or forced to resign, were guilty of miscellaneous breaches of police conduct.

It was not until August 1867, that the Watch Committee recommended to the Town Council that the strength of the Bolton force should be brought up to the government requirement of one constable per thousand of the population. The population of Bolton at the 1861 Census was approximately 70,396, so this required a force of some seventy constables. The

---

[12] *Bolton Borough Police: Dismissal Book, 1839-42,* (Bolton Archives Department).

recommendation was finally approved the following year. It was recognised even in the early years of policing, that before the police could expect respect and co-operation from the public, they must earn it.

Police Operations and their Effectiveness.

It would be reasonable to acknowledge that the physical presence of the uniformed policeman on the streets did deter some petty theft from shops and stalls, but empirical evidence of the situation is impossible to obtain. However, the 'new' police could demonstrate their effectiveness by publishing the 'statistics' of apprehensions. The easiest arrests to make were those for petty public order offences, such as begging, drunk and disorderly, drunk and incapable, illegal street- trading and soliciting. All these offences were committed in the street and were readily observed by the beat policeman. Dealing forcefully with groups such as drunks and prostitutes was popular with the 'genteel' middle-classes whose sentiments were increasingly dominant in Victorian urban society. The Watch Committee in Bolton seems to have been instrumental in issuing instructions to the superintendent regarding those offences to be scrutinised, as the following extract from 1844 indicates:

3rd April 1844: Writing or using obscene language in the streets
3rd July 1844: Suppress Public Trading.
7th August 1844: Seize all hoops from boys found bowling them in the streets.[13]

Walton provides further examples of police intervention; 'The players and spectators of street games were prosecuted for obstruction, trespass, breaches of the peace, vagrancy and desecration of the Sabbath'.[14] One inescapable fact emerges from an examination of the operations of the police in Bolton over the period; the overriding influence of the Watch Committee on the day-to-day functioning of the force. This was exercised through the office of superintendent. Carolyn Steedman sees the root of this as very firmly in the operating of an employment contract; 'municipal governments, through their Watch Committee, kept firm control of their police, and the relationship was very much that of master and servant'.[15]

The London Commissioners were reluctant to employ men in plain clothes because of concern that the 'new' police should not be reminiscent of a 'continental spy' system. Yet, it

---

[13] *Bolton Watch Committee Minute Book, 1844*, (Bolton Archives Department).
[14] Walton, *Lancashire*, p.193.
[15] C. Steedman, *Policing and the Victorian Community*, 1984, pp. 15-16.

emerges that as early as the Luddite Riots of 1810-13, Bolton police already had a 'spy' network in operation, apparently with the blessings of the magistrates. The police in Bolton also appear to have been monitoring working class drinking patterns, by their restrictions on pubs and beer-houses in the town. One reason why police officers were disliked at street level by working class people was that 'they (the police), were seen as a Government instrument by which to monitor trade union and political activity by the working-class'.[16] Hostility to constables in the execution of their duties did not always stop at verbal threats and abuse.

---

[16] R.D. Storch, 'The plague of blue locusts: Police reform and popular resistance in Northern England, 1840-57', *International Review of Social History*, xx, (1975).

Brutal Assault on Police

'Thomas Glynn, 41 and Edward Lyons, 22, were indicted for a most brutal and unmanly assault upon Robert Murray and other police constables, whilst in the execution of their duty on the 11th inst. The Recorder said that if the police were not supported in the execution of their duties, it was impossible to preserve the peace of the town. Lyons seemed to have originated the disturbances and he was sentenced to nine months and Glynn to three months in prison'.[17]

Much of the time spent on operational duties by the Bolton police appears to have covered petty offences and drink-related incidents. Alcohol was cheap and with so many unemployed, solace was sought in strong drink. The early Bolton police practised little by way of crime prevention. If the offender was not arrested at the scene of a crime then he or she stood every chance of escaping justice, unless information was forthcoming from informers or witnesses. Officers could not expect assistance and would frequently have to face active obstruction from bystanders. An examination of the statistics of arrests for police obstruction and assault gives some indication of the extent of resentment to police authority.

---

[17] *Bolton Chronicle, 24th December, 1852*, p. 4.

Table 1 (i)
Offences of Obstruction and Assault on Police: 1857-67

Year	Arrests	Discharges	Convictions	Trial
1857	18	6	8	4
1858	24	4	18	2
1859	27	4	19	4
1860	21	0	21	0
1861	32	1	31	0
1862	36	1	35	0
1863	41	5	36	0
1864	28	0	28	0
1865	31	6	25	0
1866	18	1	17	0
1867	38	8	30	0

Source: Bolton Borough Police Returns: 1857-1867, (Bolton Archives Department).

The issue of mass agitation is usually regarded as the 'principle' element in Victorian public order. The spectre of Chartism manifested itself during the period from 1839 to 1848. The role of the police in all these proceedings is an ambiguous one. In Bolton, it is difficult to judge the actual influence of the police. Throughout the period, extensive rioting was met by military force. There is little or no evidence to suggest that the police were able to handle mass action by themselves.

In the 1839 and 1842 Chartist agitation, Bolton's overstretched police were forced to request assistance from the military in Manchester. It is no coincidence that the end of Chartism is seen as the beginning of social order which corresponds with the arrival of the professional police. It is difficult to measure the effectiveness of crime prevention. Whig historians of the police, like the police reformers, lauded the new system and asserted its success. However, contemporary newspapers often carried complaints that the police were not around when they were most needed, either to prevent crime or to help victims apprehend offenders. Among the historians of crime and policing, the more critical and thoughtful have suggested that the 'new police contributed to the statistical decline of theft and violence in the second half of the nineteenth century'.[18] From the available statistics for Bolton over the period from 1857 to 1867, it does appear that in the years prior to 1860, the police were of limited efficiency and not too discreet in their efforts to maintain law and order in the town. From 1860 onwards, there is a noticeable improvement in efficiency in terms of the conviction rate, even for petty offences.

The early years of 'new' policing in Bolton are characterised by a small but rapidly changing force of men. Lack of continuity combined with injudicious appointment and remuneration as well as patent inadequacies in certain individual cases, does not support the view of an efficient force. The failure to maintain the police-population ratio and the increase in the crime rate cast further doubt on the impact of the town's police force.

Only in the late 1850s are there positive signs of improvements in efficiency. It is tempting - but perhaps misleading - to interpret police work primarily in terms of major crimes or major threats to public order. For the most part, policing in the nineteenth century was more mundane and had to include enforcing local bye-laws and dealing with petty offenders. Boys playing on the footpaths, kite flying, stone throwing, noises in the streets, troublesome dogs and vagrants were the issues to which police attention was drawn by the Watch Committees.

Two facts are worth emphasising. Firstly, the creation of an effective police force took many years. Despite the rapid growth of Bolton's population and fear of many in and around the town, limited resources were devoted to policing for well over a decade. Secondly, there is little evidence to suggest that the 'new' police in Bolton had a great impact on crime itself in the early years of the nineteenth century. The qualitative evidence of the Watch Committee Minutes does not suggest any

---

[18] V.A.C. Gatrell, 'The decline of theft and violence in Victorian and Edwardian England', in Gatrell, Lenman and Parker (eds), *Crime and the Law: The Social History of Crime in Western Europe since 1500,* (1980), pp. 277-8.

improvement in the effect of policing on Bolton and neither does the evidence indicate a great concern by the working class themselves. This tends to suggest either a higher level of tolerance of criminal behaviour in the 1840s and 1850s, or a lack of awareness of the possibilities of reducing crime. It is significant to note that it is only with the arrival of a new Chief Constable, Thomas Beech in 1867, that there are any references to the inadequacies of the police force in relation to the needs of the town. The town's rapid and industrial development, for all but the latter end of the 1850s, did not elicit a corresponding commitment to, and improvement in, policing.

Chapter Two:
The Criminal Environment

Contemporaries who thought and wrote about crime in nineteenth century Britain perceived it largely as an urban problem. Most of the more alarming and certainly the best published of crimes were committed in London. Yet, despite the dominance of the metropolis, students of crime looked beyond London and found crime in the burgeoning urban environments, with their anonymous populations and their uneducated, nomadic poor. The attempts of various sociologists and social anthropologists to explain the differences between 'rural' and 'urban' life styles, has given a theoretical underpinning to the belief that rural crime and urban crime are markedly different.

It has been suggested that in 'traditional' society, generally equated with rural society, people lived in a face-to-face community where social mobility was low, and customs and traditions legitimated. Modern society, in contrast, was viewed as impersonal and a variety of voluntary-founded associations regulated different aspects of social life. Social instability, particularly resulting from the disruption or disappearance of value systems in the new cities and towns of the nineteenth century, has been popular in explaining the growth of crime during the great period of industrialisation and urbanisation.

It is believed that environment dictates the form and styles of crime. However, some historians have detected more significant differences between rural and urban crime. Rural society, it has been argued, being more primitive, had a higher incidence of inter-personal crime than did the urban areas. In the latter, the disorganisation created by urban growth, or simply the greater opportunities for theft provided by the urban environment, led to a greater increase in property crime.

Almost half of all recorded convictions in Bolton over the ten-year period from 1857 to 1867 were drink-related. This suggests that Bolton did have a serious social problem associated with alcohol abuse. The Rev. John Clay, Chaplain of Preston Gaol stressed the relationship between drink and criminal behaviour when he wrote, 'I find that at least 35% of all crime must be put down to drinking in beer-houses and public houses'.[19] Bolton's public houses and beer-houses proliferated throughout the nineteenth century. In 1841, there were 184 beer-houses and 105 public houses, and according to the Bolton Directory for 1853, the number had increased to 192 beer-houses and 118 public houses. Within the centre of Bolton and along the three main roads, the same Directory shows that, in public houses alone, there were nine in Churchgate, twenty-six in Bradshawgate and eleven in Deansgate. This gives a total of forty-six public houses with an average distance of five hundred yards between each.

The beer-houses were licensed to sell beers only, under the terms of the Beer Act of 1830. This piece of legislation was a deliberate attempt by the government to wean the working class off the habit of 'gin-drinking', the downfalls of which were realistically portrayed by the eighteenth- century painter William Hogarth, especially in his famous painting 'Gin Lane'. However, gin continued to be drunk by the working class well into the nineteenth century. The 1830 Act provided that anyone who had a spare room and could afford a few shillings for the licence, might lawfully sell beers to the public. Unlike the public houses, the police did not supervise the beer-houses and consequently, the magistrates were virtually powerless to stop their rapid expansion. In 1845, there were 191 such beer-houses within the Borough of Bolton. It is quite easy to overlook the fact that the pub did have some socially-beneficial features. Often it provided the only means of escape from the dull toil and depressing surroundings for the working population. It was also the only place where groups, clubs and societies could meet. In fact, many workmen were forced to meet in pubs to collect their wages.

These were often paid to one man in a large sum, so his work-mates were forced to cash the note across the bar in order to divide it into smaller denominations. Gatrell and Hadden carried out an analysis by correlating the figures of convictions for assault and drunkenness with the business cycle, to show slight increases in those offences during years of prosperity. This they maintain, suggests that high wages and high employment led to a greater consumption of alcohol and this in turn, contributed to more violent crime.[20]

---

[19] *Parliamentary Papers: Select Committee on Public Houses*, (1828), vol 37, q 3714.
[20] V.A.C. Gatrell and T.B. Hadden, 'Criminal statistics and their interpretation', in E.A in Wrigley (ed), *Nineteenth century society; Essays in the use of*

In an attempt to pursue similar lines of enquiry to those by Gatrell and Hadden, the figures for assault and drink-related convictions in Bolton have been analysed to take account of local periods of trade depression (1) and those of relative prosperity (2).

Table 2 (i)
Local Trade Cycles and Convictions for Assault and Drink-Related Offences: Bolton – 1857-1867

Year	Assault	Drink-Related Offences
1857 (1)	163	252
1861 (1)	203	684
1863 (1)	87	573
1864 (1)	270	713
1865 (2)	154	680
1867 (2)	188	662

The figures suggest that Bolton exhibited a pattern quite different to that suggested by Gatrell and Hadden. The period of distress and depression (1861-64) show increases in drink-related convictions and assault, whilst the periods of relative prosperity (1865-67) show actual decreases in assault but little overall change in those drink-related offences. These figures leave two possible conclusions to be drawn.

Either assaults were not as closely linked to drink as the authors have suggested, or Bolton's working-class saw drink as an integral part of their culture. However, this does not entirely negate the generally accepted view of the relationship between drink and violence. There is little doubt that in times of extreme hardship, Bolton's working-class sought solace in drink and the resultant assaults were a further manifestation of despair and apathy. This is particularly true for 1864 which witnessed increases in both offences.

All participants in the discussion of crime and its causes can agree on one point, that drink was a prominent factor. Many of the public houses and beer-houses in the town were patronised by the working-class throughout the day. The breakdown of times of arrest for drink-related offences reveal a clear pattern (Table 2 (ii)). The majority of offences took place between 11 p.m. and 2 a.m. Pubs served as an unobtrusive agent

---

quantitative methods for the study of social data (Cambridge, 1972), pp. 370-71., pp. 370-71.

in the criminal life of Bolton. Their greatest number being concentrated in the poorer areas of the town facilitated this. By today's standards, the availability of drinking establishments and the number of persons engaged in the drink trade was extraordinary. It is of relevance that the pressure and propaganda of the Temperance Movement and the religious bodies did not reduce the number of publicans or pubs; they merely brought a temporary halt to their expansion.[22]

Table 2 (ii)
Number of Afternoon Drunkards Arrested: Bolton 1860

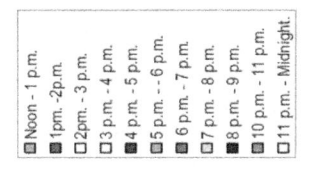

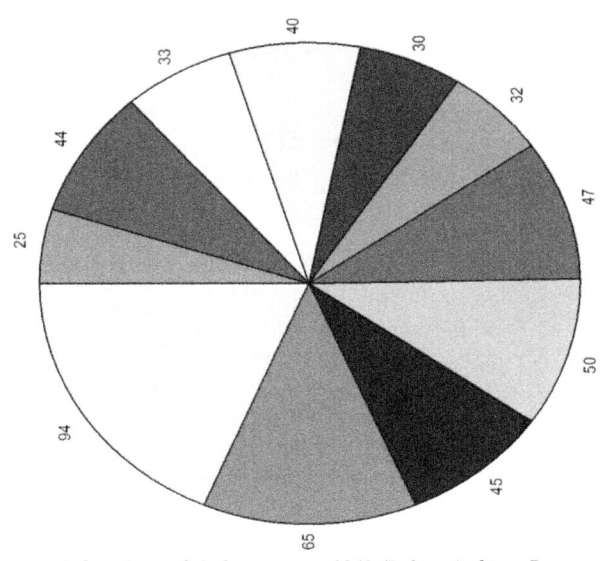

Source: Bolton Borough Police returns: 1860 (Bolton Archives Department).

It is clear that there was considerable opposition to the beer trade from Bolton town officials:

LICENSING DAY AT BOLTON – 24th AUGUST 1848

'Report by Mr John Taylor, Coroner of the Borough, in opposition to the granting of Licences.

There were 96 Inns in Great Bolton and in Little Bolton 20; there were also beer-houses in Great Bolton totalling 125, Little Bolton 66. There was a drinking place for every 25 locals or one for every 200 souls. Twelve of the inns, the publicans have been fined or reprimanded for offences which have been committed on the Sabbath; eight were known places at which gaming was permitted; at twelve, known prostitutes were permitted to assemble. Out of the 68 Inquests held up to August this year, 23 deaths have been directly attributed to drinking. Of the 90-100 public houses already licensed, 30 are to be found within the space of 300 yards, and within the distance of the Parish Church. Churchgate is one black mass of public houses. No new licences were granted this year.'[21]

The rapid increase in arrests for drink-related offences, especially after mid-century, indicates an increase in police vigilance:

'The Returns do not indicate any improvement in consequence of the misconduct of some members of the trade, more particularly amongst some of the beer-sellers that have caused a stricter and more extensive surveillance of the police. The selling at prohibited hours is cause for much concern as it is the cause also of much drunkenness and disorderly conduct on the Sabbath day. The greatest amount of crime committed in the Borough generally originates in beer-houses, and is committed by

---

[21] J. Taylor, *Autobiography of a Lancashire Lawyer*, (Bolton, 1883), pp. 360-71.

persons of the lowest class of society, who resort to such houses.'[22]

One of the major causes of drunkenness among women had been the purchases of alcoholic beverages from grocers and other off-licence establishments. It appears that such a change in drinking habits would give rise to less respectable drinking places, which were beyond the jurisdiction of the licensing laws and catered to a more vicious clientele. Drunkenness was a serious problem in Bolton, particularly on Sunday and almost always exclusively involved the working class.

Sunday was the only day when they had free time for recreation and, after they had spent six days working the factory, the pub was a welcome relaxation. Sunday was also the day when the 'respectable' citizens travelled into the town centre to worship. The meeting of these two social classes often ended in disaster. 'Churchgoers were mocked and sometimes spat on by drunkards'.[23] It was common for men to spend an entire weeks' wages in the pub, leaving nothing for the family to live on until the next payday. This situation often led to desertion, violence and the need for parish relief. Many contemporaries offered reasons for the cause of drunkenness; lack of education, weakness of character, unemployment and bad companions, but few really understood the compulsive nature of alcoholism and the hold it had on people's lives.

---

[22] *Bolton Chief Constable's Report to the Watch Committee, October 1860*, (Bolton Archives Department).
[23] R. Poole, Leisure in Bolton, (Lancaster, 1982), p.91.

Lodging-Houses and Pawnbrokers.

Common lodging-houses have been defined as 'those in which persons are harboured or lodged for hire, for a single night or for less than a week at a time'.[24] Many who engaged in criminal activities lived in lodging-houses. This institution in its many forms was a distinctive part of the poorer neighbourhoods of Bolton during the nineteenth century and grew in response to the sizeable population of young and unattached persons. While lodging-houses mushroomed as a result of demographic pressures, they represented at the same time a kind of 'permissive society', in which strangers mixed together in an atmosphere free from the conventions of the respectable classes.

The permissive nature of lodging-houses is particularly emphasised by Goslin:

'To give a commentary on the general disregard for the law and widespread immorality of the Bolton of the 1830s and 1840s, it is recorded that there were over sixty low lodging-houses in which the sexes were able to sleep together with carefree abandon, in common rooms'.[25]

There was a tendency for the police to label certain lodging-house districts as criminal and concentrate their attention there:

'The greatest part of crime and depredation are committed either directly or indirectly by such characters (tramps and vagrants) who either commit it themselves or make the necessary observation and communicate the same to a common thief whom they have arranged to meet at the house of lodging at night'.[26]

Lodging-houses with their rootless, generally single population were suspect at least from the 1750s. Angus Reach reported that the Chief Constable of Manchester spoke of 'a considerable floating population, and a smaller number of

---

[24] L.W. Kershaw, *Justice's Note Book*, (London, 1908), p.91.
[25] Goslin, *Duty Bound*, p.24.
[26] *Bolton Borough Police: Chief Constable's Report to the Watch Committee, October,1855*, (Bolton Archives Department).

persons who are known both to work and steal'.[27] The figures for Bolton suggest that in 1853, there were a total of some eighty-four lodging houses within the town centre. It was only after the Watch Committee issued Rules for the Regulation of Lodging-Houses in the Borough in 1851 that noticeable reductions were seen:

Table 2 (iii)
Lodging-Houses in the Borough of Bolton: 1853-1867

1853	84	1857	45	1861	31	1865	29
1854	63	1858	41	1862	43	1866	19
1855	50	1859	45	1863	35	1867	19
1856	44	1860	41	1864	32		

Source: Bolton Borough Police: Chief Constable's Reports- 1853-67, (Bolton Archives Department).

A proportion of Bolton's offenders were no doubt to be found in the lodging-house districts, given that over 23% of the town's population resided there. Lodging-houses, unlike pubs, back streets and isolated places, were rarely scenes of crime in Bolton, but they did serve to bring together the 'criminal classes'. Thieves, tramps and vagrants, in addition to prostitutes, all took up lodging in cellars and cheap lodging-houses. 'To this end, the lodging-house became a symbol of unrespectability, it provided an unchallenged incubator for disease, filth and immorality'.[28]

Pawnbrokers were important figures to the urban working-class communities of the eighteenth and nineteenth centuries; they provided a vital financial service within these communities and not simply to the casual labourer. Sometimes, certain kinds of goods were left with the pawnbroker on a regular weekly basis; good clothes could be pawned during the week and redeemed for weekends after pay-day. Many of the articles of clothing, bed-linen, table-linen and cutlery taken in petty theft were also hastened to the pawnbroker.

They were the mainstay of the poorest neighbourhoods in Bolton and were termed the 'poor man's bank' in that they produced the sources of supply of ready cash for household and personal articles. The level of pawnbroking was also an indicator of the economic condition of the community. During times of hardship, many people visited the pawnshop as a means of

---

[27] J. Ginswick, *Labour and the Poor*, vol 1, p.39.
[28] C.M. de-Motte, '*The Dark Side of Town: Crime in Manchester and Salford, 1815-75*'(unpublished Ph.D. Thesis, University of Kansas, 1977), p.200.

avoiding starvation or the workhouse. Generally, the pawnshop was as much a part of the physical environment as were stalls, pubs and shops.

'Insecurity of income and the physical conditions of life combined to produce a distinct outlook of which pawning was an integral part'. [29]

Pawnshops increased with the growth of population and were well-scattered throughout the poorest areas of Bolton. Apart from the suspect pawnbrokers, plunder often passed to dealers in second-hand goods and marine stores. Criminal operations always needed a network of institutions through which illicit goods and services could be provided. Therefore, it was quite natural that the Bolton criminal underworld made use of these existing institutions.

Table 2 (iv)
Pawnbrokers in Bolton: 1853-1870

1853	26	1859	20	1865	33
1854	22	1860	22	1866	33
1855	21	1861	24	1867	34
1856	14	1862	28	1868	32
1857	23	1863	32	1869	32
1858	24	1864	31	1870	37

Source: Bolton Borough Police Returns: 1853-1870 (Bolton Archives Department).

The figures for Bolton reveal that the pawnbroker was very much an integral part of working-class life in the town during the nineteenth century. The majority of pawnshops were located in the town centre. This area also contained the greatest concentration of Irish and working-class families. The pledge

---

[29] M. Tebbutt, '*Making Ends Meet': Pawnbroking and Working Class Credit,* (Leicester, 1983), p.19.

shop was regarded as a safe repository for other valuables as well as money; married couples at work all day left goods there in case their homes were burgled. Residents of lodging-houses were particularly vulnerable to theft, and they too left their goods at the pledge shop in preference to premises where there were many transients.

The Select Committee of 1870 investigating pawn-broking, revealed the extent to which even the most respectable traders ignored regulations. Legal amendments to the 1800 Act had merely legitimated existing charges or introduced new possibilities for abuse. The custom of making a ticket charge on small loans was recognised in 1860, when a half-penny fee was introduced for sums less than five shillings. Police enforcement was largely preoccupied with the trade's criminal dimension which came under increasing scrutiny as the Bolton force endeavoured to increase their general anti-criminal measures - and attempted to implement intrusive powers of search and inspection over the trade's books. These invariably clashed with the trade's desires for commercial legitimacy. It is quite evident that not all police viewed the pawn-broking trade as suspect:

> 'As far as my experience goes, I can say that the number of instances in which stolen goods are offered in pledge, bears such a small proportion to the total transactions over the pledge counter as to be utterly insignificant'.[30]

Nevertheless, it is a fact that the trade was a more likely outlet for the occasional thief than the professional criminal. Goods stolen from shops and stalls in Bolton's town centre, especially on Market days, would invariably find their way to the pawnshop. It is more likely that initially, the goods would be deposited with a recognised 'handler' who would then attempt to dispose of the items through a known pawnshop (for a fee, of course). A casual acceptance of pledges without proper questioning meant that the pawnbrokers tacitly connived in criminal transactions, while the frequent discrepancy between the cost price of a stolen article and its pledge value tended to fuel popular suspicion of the trade as a whole.

---

[30] J. Caminada, *Twenty-Five Years of Detective Life*, (Manchester, 1895), Reprint (1982), pp. 34-36.

Criminal Neighbourhoods

Rural society was more primitive and therefore displayed a higher incidence of inter-personal crime than urban areas. In the latter, the disorganisation created by urban growth or simply the greater opportunity for theft provided by the urban environment, led to a greater incidence of property crime. Not every residential district was prone to crime, but some were notorious. Irish districts in particular were singled out as primarily criminal:

> 'Some and not simply Irish districts became virtual 'no-go' areas for the police and more particularly, for the rent collector and landlord'.[31]

It may be that there was a high level of theft within such districts, which was never reported because of the inhabitant's antipathy to the police. Victims might also be intimidated against bringing charges, and this was one reason why criminal statistics underestimated the undoubted criminality of Bolton's poorer districts. In some respects, certain residential areas, especially where the landlords and rent collectors dared not enter, and where repairs were never made to property, may have been worse in respect of poverty and squalor than those districts of the town with lodging-houses.

Environment did interact with crime, but not simply along the lines that the urban/rural divide suggests. During the eighteenth and nineteenth centuries, industrialisation and urbanisation had an impact on communities. Some of these tended to be more law-abiding than others, but theorists of crime, policemen and the 'respectable' classes in general, tended to perceive any areas where the poor teemed, as potential havens for the 'criminal classes'.

Popular disorder, even when it had recognisable and even modest aims such as food at a fair price or a fair wage, was increasingly perceived as dangerous and criminal. Popular exuberance at the town's market and fairs, and the noise and disorder spilling over from the numerous town-centre pubs, were also perceived as potential threats to good order.

---

[31] D. Englander, *Landlord and Tenant in Urban Britain,* (Oxford, 1983), pp. 34-36.

Prostitution and Vagrancy

Women constituted about 24% of Bolton's criminal population, as evidenced by the number of males and females arrested during the period 1851 to 1870. Many of these women engaged in prostitution, often working in concert with men and thieves, but not wholly averse to working alone whenever the opportunity presented itself. Robbery and pick-pocketing were the commonest forms of crime with which prostitutes were associated. Prostitution, which in the eighteenth century had been a rather casual trade, being centred on the 'loose' taverns and lodging-houses, later took on a more organised form and was carried out in numerous brothels organised by women.

The Bolton Police Returns for 1844 refer to thirty brothels in the town, while the following year, the Returns refer to 'Houses where prostitutes reside' rather than to 'brothels', and this latter format appears to have been adopted in all subsequent Police Returns. During local Wakes and fairs, there was considerable competition in Bolton from visiting 'professionals' from Manchester, competing for trade with the Bolton locals. Among the local street walkers, the trade was quite often followed by several members of the same family. Many such families became social outcasts, living on the fringe, usually possessing long court records involving bastardy, drunkenness, assault and theft.

Prostitution itself was not a criminal offence, but there was growing concern about the 'great social evil' and determined attempts were made to rescue these 'fallen women':

> 'There has been a considerable decrease in the number of apprehensions of 'unfortunate women'. This may in some degree be attributed to the efforts of a number of philanthropic gentlemen who, in laudable manner, sought out these women and succeeded in placing a number of them in institutions which have, for their object, the rescuing of this class of young offenders from further degradation'.[32]

It is significant that for women transported for theft in the early nineteenth century, the designations 'hardened

---

[32] *Bolton Borough Police Chief Constable's Report to the Watch Committee, October 1868*, (Bolton Archives Department).

offender' and 'abandoned prostitutes' were almost synonymous. Several of the social investigators who studied prostitution noted that economic hardship was a spur for some women to take up 'the profession'. Tobias portrays the women of the criminal class as 'primarily the aiders and abettors of their men folk'.[33]

Some prostitutes did in fact rob their clients, although the reluctance of victims to come forward in such circumstances was not unusual. The majority of crimes committed by women and girls in the nineteenth century were associated with prostitution. Prostitution reached epidemic proportions, especially in the large towns and cities such as Manchester and Liverpool. The slight increase during the depression years of 1862 to 1864 suggests that unemployment and economic necessity forced some women 'on the town'. In one sense, prostitution was a demographic phenomenon. In Bolton, the numbers of women exceeded that of men in practically every district of the town; the 1861 Census Returns show 32,638 males and 36,660 females. To say that the industrial system created the position would be a crude over-simplification. However, there is some validity in the argument that economic hardship brought on by unemployment and low wages, contributed to prostitution, and all were side effects of industrial life.

Even in the heart of textile Lancashire that traditionally employed more women than other areas, there was nevertheless a lack of employment outlets for women in the nineteenth century. The brothel provided the dual function of housing prostitutes and giving them a place to promote their trade. Chief Constables' Reports to Watch Committees indicate that a fair number of beer-houses were sometimes used as fronts for prostitution:

> 'A brothel or back-street lodging, with frequent gentlemen callers, was a haven of luxury compared to the normal basement kitchen or a cheerless attic'.[34]

The prostitutes themselves were usually thieves, if for no other reason than their 'profession' provided an easy cover for larceny. They would on many occasions work in teams to commit robberies. They would pick the pockets of clients when

---

[33] J.J. Tobias, *Crime and Industrial Society in the Nineteenth Century*, (Harmondsworth, 1972), pp. 103-7.
[34] F. Finnegan, *Poverty and Prostitution: A Study of Victorian Prostitutes in York*, (Cambridge, 1979), pp. 117-124.

they were the worse for drink and property thus stolen would quickly pass to a seller of stolen goods. During the day they would call at pubs and at night visit the theatres. Many prostitutes lived with a man or had a protector, so it was only natural that they would have a working relationship in crime as well. They were prone to live in certain neighbourhoods with familiar company in old haunts. They knew the streets and alleys and could use them to good effect in escaping from the police or the victims of their robberies. This would be one indication that they were, in general, local to Bolton and not outsiders.

Most of the Bolton street-walkers operated a well-defined route within the town, usually taking in the busy thoroughfares of Deansgate and Bradshawgate. In this area were located numerous dwellings in the small courts and alleys, which doubled as brothels. In the middle years of the nineteenth century, there was a general feeling among the middle-class that crime and vice were on the increase in Bolton.

In 1840, James Slade, Vicar of Bolton, wrote to the Trustees of Great Bolton voicing this concern:

> 'We are deeply concerned to hear of the great increase of vice and crime in this town, more especially at night, and the difficulty of preventing and detecting offences is much augmented by the want of sufficient light. These remarks apply in particular to the neighbourhood of the Manchester and Bolton railway station, where a number of loose and disorderly people are very frequently collected for their evil purposes. Other parts of the town are also exposed to similar irregularities and mischief'.[35]

Prostitution as such was not a criminal offence; the prostitution offences were specifically soliciting, living off immoral earnings and running 'houses of ill-repute', although these were enforced selectively by the police. Women soliciting on the streets appear to have been most vulnerable to prosecution, particularly during the period in which the Contagious Diseases Act remained on the Statute Book (1864,1866,1869).

---

[35] *Letter from Rev. J. Slade, Vicar of Bolton to the Trustees of Great Bolton, dated 3rd February 1854,* (Bolton Archives Department).

Table 2 (v)
Offences of Prostitution: Bolton 1857-67

Year	Arrests	Convictions	Trial	Known prostitutes
1857	26	16	0	62
1858	17	6	0	61
1859	32	17	0	71
1860	28	24	0	80
1861	24	28	0	87
1862	14	12	0	84
1863	16	13	2	82
1864	32	31	1	91
1865	35	30	3	98
1866	34	31	1	94
1867	43	39	4	87

Source: *Bolton Borough Police Returns: 1853-1870, (Bolton Archives Department).*

The fact that prostitution accounted for only 2% of all convictions suggests that these offences were not as prominent a feature of criminal activity in the town as has been suggested. There were some years when there appears to have been an increase in both arrests and convictions, particularly in 1864, 1866 and 1867. Those years were relatively prosperous in terms of employment, so the correlation between economic necessity and prostitution is questionable. However, many families and individuals suffered from the long-term effects of economic fluctuation. Even in relatively good years, many still experienced unemployment and desertion, both factors reducing them to poverty level.

What is of particular significance is that the high numbers of prostitutes known to the Bolton police and the subsequent percentages of actual arrests, suggest that the police did in fact exercise a certain degree of discretion when this was left to them. There is also the fact that many of the street-walkers who were aware of police surveillance would resort to the many beer-houses available in the town. The apparent increases in arrests in the mid-1860s is a reflection of the particular firm stand taken by the town's magistrates and reinforced through the Watch Committee.

The significant numbers of prostitutes being sent for trial after 1863 does suggest that they had probably committed more than just offences connected with prostitution - probably theft and assault. It is obvious from the figures that the magistrates appear to have been particularly concerned with preserving a rather narrowly defined morality in the town, especially when these figures are compared with those for drink-related offences.

During the eighteenth century, young men in their late teens and early twenties were often living-in apprentices or servants of various kinds. Some may have been tempted into crime to obtain money to support their leisure activities and to establish a degree of independence alongside their peers, especially in those difficult years waiting before full independence as a tradesman. Some absconded or were thrown out by their master and were, in consequence, unable to use the local employment market. Their existence became, at least for a while, marginal; they were forced to move on looking for work. Vagrants were invariably eyed with suspicion and the labelling process of 'vagrant' being synonymous with 'thief' could become self-fulfilling.

Habitual tramps became beggars first, then thieves and finally convicts. In early Victorian Bolton, like most other townships, beggars were sometimes ubiquitous, ingenious and colourful characters. The streets and thoroughfares contained a whole section of the population who lived by soliciting alms from passers-by. Some claimed to be ex-sailors and army veterans, others said that they were distressed operatives. There were 'artists' who chalked on the pavement and sellers of matches and bootlaces. They were of all ages and of both sexes, and their object was to trade on the consciences of other more fortunate residents.

> 'The number of tramps or vagrants passing through the town has decreased this year to 2,165. The greater part of this number is a population very dangerous to society, such as gypsies, beggars, strollers and thieves, which all villages, large and small, market towns and cities are more or less annually annoyed with.'[36]

> 'I know from personal observation, that it is quite common for one tramp to tell another the exploits of

---

[36] *Bolton Borough Police: Chief Constable's Report for October 1854.* (Bolton Archives Department).

the day, at the same time informing him of the most charitable houses in the area, describing the different houses to be called at and the venues, persons and hours to be waited on. Perhaps the sympathy of the inexperienced may lead them to criticise the conduct of the police in such cases, but I can assure such innocent sympathising minds, that the greatest part of crime and depredation are committed either directly or indirectly by such characters' [37]

Table 2 (vi) Vagrancy

Year	Arrests	Discharges	Convictions	% of Arrests
1857	77	75	2	3
1858	17	13	4	24
1859	20	20	0	0
1860	10	4	6	60
1861	46	39	7	11
1862	38	33	5	13
1863	48	40	8	17
1864	47	47	0	0
1865	10	2	8	80
1866	27	20	7	26
1867	19	15	4	21

Source: Bolton Borough Police Returns: 1857-1870, (Bolton Archives department).

The very low conviction rate over the period suggests that vagrancy in Bolton was dealt with more as a nuisance than as a crime, with convictions standing at approximately 23% of arrests. Both 1860 and 1865 show a higher than usual conviction rate which does appear consistent with the concerns voiced by the Chief Constable who, in turn, echoed the wishes of the Watch Committee.

---

[37] *Bolton Borough Police: Chief Constable's Report for October 1853.* (Bolton Archives Department).

Theft of Property and Juvenile Crime

The criminal element as a whole was perceived as predominantly male, to the extent that statistically, women appear to have committed fewer thefts. However, the difficulty arises in that the available statistical data covers all offences not just theft, so there is no reliable evidence of women's role in theft-related offences.

Table 2 (vii)
Comparison of Male and Female Arrests

Year	Male	%	Female	%	Total Arrests
1854	2,009	77	591	23	2,600
1855	1,869	75	624	25	2,493
1856	1,485	74	521	26	2,006
1857	1,375	76	441	24	1,816
1858	1,433	76	458	24	1,891
1859	1,660	74	578	26	2,238
1860	1,591	71	646	29	2,237
1861	1,712	75	565	25	2,277
1862	1,421	74	496	26	1,917
1863	1,616	74	564	26	2,180
1864	1,524	74	537	26	2,061
1865	1,616	73	597	27	2,213
1866	1,656	76	513	24	2,169
1867	2,816	81	663	19	3,479
1868	2,892	80	732	20	3,624
1869	2,198	76	681	24	2,879
1870	2,370	77	699	23	3,069

Source: *Bolton Borough Police Returns: 1850-1870, (Bolton Archives Department).*

The statistics and court records suggest that the overwhelming majority of thefts reported and prosecuted were opportunist and petty. The greatest number of offenders arrested and imprisoned was always drawn from the ranks of young men. Clearly, not all young men arrested for crimes in their teens and early twenties carried on with a criminal 'career' in later life. Crime in the form of thefts committed by men from the poorer sections of the working class was transitory behaviour, possibly fostered by economic hardship and encouraged by opportunity.

It would appear that larceny per se, was a random form of behaviour, whereby the contacts between thief and victim owed as much to the latter's misfortune as to anything else.

In effect, larceny followed certain patterns and could be characterised by the place where thefts occurred. Thieves tended to operate in places where people and their possessions would be most vulnerable. Considering the amount of time people in Bolton spent in public-houses and beer-houses, it is inevitable that these places would become fertile ground for theft. In cases of robbery from the person, thieves often placed themselves in the commercial centre of the town around Deansgate and Bradshawgate, where the chances of acquiring considerable sums of money would be enhanced. Such thieves would loiter around banks and estate offices in wait for men and women with considerable purses.

Usually thieves would take advantage of the drunken condition of public house patrons, especially on market days, and plunder them at will. Theft from shops by both insiders and outsiders was another problem in Bolton. This was partly the result of misplaced trust by employers acting in good faith, putting irresistible temptation within the reach of their employees and customers alike. The arrival of the railways in Bolton after 1830, created other advantages for theft from warehouses, goods yards and the stations. The stations formed the focal point for local thieves who preyed on the numerous passengers passing through the town. Theft would be enhanced particularly during the darker afternoons of winter-time, when gas lighting was only available along the main roads and streets of the town. Quite often, many of the small courtyards and alleys shared one common gas lamp, so there were ample dark areas in which to make good an escape.

There is the assumption that theft in the form of burglary from a warehouse is different from theft in the form of pilferage by a warehouseman. 'Fiddling' between business men is still one of the most common forms of fraud and was the most common in the nineteenth century. The key question however, is to what extent did the massive changes brought about in the workplace bring about changes in workplace crime?

Coal miners were allowed coal for their own use, and any movement of goods not directly supervised offered employees the opportunity for fraud. On the canals, the boatmen removed cloth, ironmongery, liquor, sugar and tea, indeed anything which could be turned to their own use or sold off to a receiver. Many such receivers were grocers, others were manufacturers who took goods and sold them as their own. The replacement of canal transport by the railway did not abolish such pilfering, it simply changed its location. During the eighteenth century, coal-mine owners often loaded more coal into barges than the barge weight, but also because they were well aware that the boatmen 'sold coal en route and paid off lock-keepers and other officials'.[38]

Other employers tolerated 'fiddles' which did not hit them personally, but which could be passed onto the buyer. At the end of the nineteenth century, dairy owners admitted that they took the dishonesty of their milkmen into account when calculating wages. The most common fiddle was 'bobbing' or watering down the milk and selling the surplus at a profit. In general, the workplace offences were those committed by employees. Several historians have sought to slot their perception of such offences into changes in the economic structure. It has, for example, been stressed that 'the shift to centralised factory-based manufacture was less the result of that system's superiority and more because of concern about embezzlement under the 'out-work' system'.[39] Such analyses have considerable attractions in that they relate changes in society and the economy to concurrent changes in the law. There is evidence for a close link between industrial development and prosecution for industrial theft.

In early nineteenth century Wigan for example, the law appears to have been administered humanely and impartially by the local magistracy, except when it involved local industry. Employers were scarcely prosecuted - and if convicted were only moderately fined for contravening the Truck Act. On the other hand, heavy sentences were imposed for first time offences of industrial theft.[40] Domestic servants might be 'tested' for honesty with coinage or paper money left where they were likely to be seen. Dismissal of a dishonest servant was of course far easier and far cheaper than seeking a prosecution. Greenwood noted that many juveniles resorted to crime because of hunger, yet in general, habitual criminals were rarely perceived as being

---

[38] H. Hanson, *The Canal Boatmen, 1760-1914*, (Manchester University Press, 1975), p.37.
[39] S.A. Marglin, 'What Do Bosses Do? The Origins and Functions of Hierarchy in Capitalist Production', *Review of Radical Political Economies, No 6* (1974), pp. 46-55.
[40] Barrett, *Crime and Punishment*,' pp. 84-86.

brought to crime through poverty. Bad, uncaring parents, drink and a general lack of moral fibre continued to be wheeled out as causes of crime.[41]

The lack of moral training was not a new phenomenon in the early nineteenth century, although it was taken up and emphasised by a group of educational reformers who were particularly concerned about juvenile crime. Individuals such as Mary Carpenter, Joseph Fletcher, James Kay-Shuttleworth and John Wade, 'urged that proper education would lead to a diminution of crime'.[42] Select Committees of Parliament as early as 1816 and 1828 presented reports on different aspects of crime, and they were particularly concerned at what seemed to be an increasing number of juvenile offenders. Witnesses blamed indigent parents who ignored their offspring, and to a lesser degree, 'shopkeepers and stall holders who foolishly expose their wares'.[43]

---

[41] J. Greenwood, T*he Seven Curses of London,* (1891), Reprint (Blackwell, Oxford, 1981), p. 57.
[42] S. Margery 'The Invention of Juvenile Delinquency in Early Nineteenth Century England', *Labour History, No 34,* (1978), pp. 56-62.
[43] *Parliamentary Papers Select Committee on the Police of the Metropolis,* (1828), (553), vi, p.57.

Table 2 (viii)

Convictions for Theft: Bolton 1857-1867

Legend:
- Larceny Miscellaneous
- Larceny Dwelling
- Larceny Person
- Embezzlement
- Robbery Person
- Fraud
- Larceny Servants

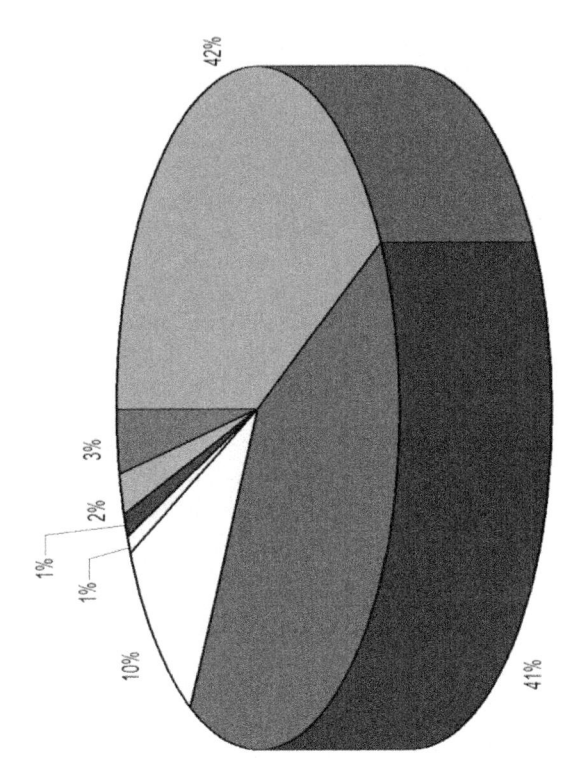

Values shown: 42%, 3%, 2%, 1%, 1%, 10%, 41%

Source: Bolton Borough Police Returns: 1850-1870 (Bolton Archives Department).

Shoplifting appears to have been a prominent feature of juvenile crime in Bolton during the nineteenth century:

'I have this year, to remark with very great satisfaction upon the decided improvement in the appearance of the stalls. It has diminished the amount of petty theft because the stalls always had many temptations and afforded considerable facilities to juveniles to commit petty theft'.[44]

Something of a consensus emerged that juvenile offenders started with petty theft and then progressed to more serious offences. However, there is insufficient statistical data to indicate the true extent of juvenile crime in Bolton during the nineteenth century. Whilst the Juvenile Offenders' Acts of 1847 and 1850 empowered magistrates to try juveniles of the ages of fourteen and sixteen for simple larceny, those convicted are not shown in Police Returns under a separate category but included in the general groupings for larceny. Within the broad category of theft, data indicates that most convictions were for miscellaneous larceny which covered petty offences; shoplifting and theft from the workplace. Burglary from dwellings appears to have been a particular feature, making up approximately 41% of all thefts.

There is little doubt that during the nineteenth century, industrialisation and urbanisation changed communities. Some communities tended to be more law-abiding than others, but theorists of crime have tended to perceive any areas where the poor lived and where there was no visible form of elite control or surveillance, as havens for the 'dangerous' classes. Popular disorder, even when it had recognisable and modest aims – food at a fair price, the traditional right to use common land – was increasingly perceived as dangerous and criminal. Popular exuberance at fairs and markets, the noise and disorder which spilled over from pubs and beer-houses, crowded courts and streets, were all viewed with suspicion and fear.

Whilst some of this disorder could be considered 'criminal' in the very narrow sense of the word, it does appear to have been difficult for those contemporaries fuelled by the Victorian ideals of 'respectability' and 'progress' to perceive the difference between criminal behaviour and community continuity.

---

[44] *Bolton Borough Police: Chief Constables Report to the Watch Committee, October 1856,* (Bolton Archives Department).

Chapter Three:
A Statistical Profile

Historians who seek to use crime figures have to confront certain challenges. Historical evidence is, by its very nature, fragmentary and simply cannot provide its own conclusions; it requires interpretation. Few historians seek to base general conclusions on one set of source material, least of all, on the statistical evidence of something whose definition is as elusive as that of crime. However, statistics used with caution provide a starting point and a hypothesis for patterns of both criminal activity and responses to perceptions of that activity.

In this chapter contemporary statistical sources are employed to test the reality of Victorian images and assumptions about urban crime as they are applied to Bolton. Even though their usefulness has been questioned, crime statistics on arrests and convictions are at least one indicator of police activity, the types of offences they faced, and who was committing the various offences. Statistics are thus a general measure of crime and police activity. Many of the key questions about crime are quantitative. What was the extent of criminal activity? Did it increase or decrease over time? What were the most prevalent types of crime? Did economic and social change influence different kinds of criminality?

There are no national crime figures available before 1805 therefore historians are faced with the task of having to consult judicial records for statistical data on indictments, trials and convictions. These are located in either Assize records at the Public Records Office or in the Quarter Sessions records housed in county record offices. It was not until 1810 that the government published figures of committals for indictable offences in England and Wales going back to 1805. From 1810 onwards, the statistics were published annually. It was during the 1830s and 1840s that the 'statistical movement' rose to prominence in Britain.

These published crime statistics were grouped into six main categories of offence, the classification being unchanged to the present day:

- Offences against the Person (from common assault to homicide).
- Offences against Property with Violence (robbery, burglary etc).
- Offences against Property without Violence (larceny, theft).
- Malicious Offences against Property (arson, machine-breaking).
- Offences against the Currency (base-coinage, counterfeiting).
- Miscellaneous Offences (from vagrancy to riot).

Offenders could be brought before three principal types of court during the nineteenth century. The least serious offences could be dealt with summarily by magistrates sitting alone or in pairs in petty sessions. The number of offences which could be tried summarily increased significantly during the nineteenth century. In the larger cities and towns such as Manchester and Liverpool, stipendiary magistrates acting in what were increasingly referred to as 'police courts', took on summary jurisdiction.

More serious offences were prosecuted on indictment and were held at Quarter Sessions which met four times a year in both county and corporate towns such as Bolton. The most serious offences, for example homicide and manslaughter, were tried before judges at assizes. During the nineteenth century there were two assizes each year, held in the major county towns of most counties at Lent and during the summer. In Lancashire, these were held in Lancaster, Liverpool and Manchester.

The major difficulty with the principal forms of criminal statistics is the 'dark figure', that is, the number of offences committed of which there is no record. Committals and indictments leave an even bigger gap between themselves and what might be hypothesised as 'the actual amount of crime'. The statistics of committals and indictments which form the basis of the criminal statistics are obviously some way from any measurement of 'actual crime'. They are the end product of a variety of filters and require at the very least, a victim prepared to prosecute, or someone prepared to report an offence and an individual who has been accused and apprehended.

Individual prosecutions were also the product of a social, economic and political context which changed from decade to decade, and even from year to year. Thus, in some years, the context may have provoked a ferocious response to a particular criminal offence, but in others the response may have been far more lenient. The succession of problems inherent in criminal statistics led Tobias to despair of their utility when he wrote, 'changes in Chief Constables produce changes in one series of figures'.[45] Tobias's concern was simply that crime statistics were just too unreliable for any value to be made of them without additional substantive evidence. Some criminologists have argued that the further a criminal record is from the original act, the less use it has for any analysis of the pattern of criminality.[46]

The figures of crime reported to the police are more significant than the figure of cases processed by the courts. Since all criminal and judicial statistics are the products of the decisions and purposes of those responsible for the control of crime, they can never be used as a measure of 'actual criminal activity'. The most significant study of nineteenth century judicial statistics for England and Wales is that by Gatrell. He argues that the national figures, taken over the long-term, iron out idiosyncrasies and freak periodic fluctuations, to give a true picture of the 'pattern' - though naturally not the 'level' of crime.[47]

---

[45] Tobias, *Crime and Industrial Society*, pp. 19-25.
[46] T. Sellin,'The Significance of the Records of Crime', *Law Quarterly Review*, Lxv, (1951), pp. 489-504.
[47] V.A.C. Gatrell, *'The Decline of Theft and Violence'*, p. 248.

Offences of the Period

Analysis of the available statistical data contained in the Chief Constables' Reports to the Bolton Watch Committee over the period from 1849 to 1880, reveal that there were nine offences which were statistically significant in terms of their arrest and conviction rates. These have been designated 'Principal Offences'. The remaining offences which are significant in terms of their conviction rates have been designated 'Miscellaneous Offences'.

Principal Offences

i. Assault

This offence included common assault resulting in some form of physical contact. Such assaults often took place in and around the public house; domestic violence and malicious wounding were also forms of inter-personal violence. Most assaults occurred between people who were related or known to each other. A degree of physical punishment meted out to dependants seems to have been accepted or at least tolerated across social groups during the nineteenth century. Masters beat their servants, husbands their wives and parents their children. However, there were limits to such assaults. Assault resulting in wounding with intent to commit grievous bodily harm or assault occasioning actual bodily harm would be included under the miscellaneous offence of Assault with Wounding. It is important here to consider the link between drink and violence. Quite often excessive drinking resulted in heated arguments.

ii. Drink-Related Offences

These comprised the offences of being drunk and incapable and drunk and causing a breach of the peace. Examination of the figures reveals that towards the closing years of the 1850s, there was a steady decline in the number of discharges and a corresponding increase in summary convictions for these offences. In addition, there are numerous references in the Chief Constables' Reports which highlight the problems posed by the conduct of both publicans and beer-house proprietors and the subsequent need for extra police surveillance of such premises.

iii. Breach of the Peace

This offence was committed where there was any threat to public order or incitement to commit such threat, including illegal street gatherings. No doubt Bolton's magistracy were mindful of the earlier outbreaks of disorder associated with Chartist agitation, which would have had some impact upon their sentencing strategy.

iv. Larceny

There were three specific offences regarding larceny; larceny in dwellings, miscellaneous larceny and larceny against the person. It must be recognised that the perceptions of victim and police could influence the labelling of an offence. The difference between robbery and larceny from the person was technically that violence was employed in the latter; but the two often overlapped and the outcome was dependent on how the victim and/ or the police wished to interpret 'violence'. A similar problem existed with burglary and some larceny; the decision to proceed with a summary prosecution or with an indictment at assizes could rest with the police perception of the accused's character, and whether or not he had previous convictions. It would appear that if the accused was 'known' to the police they would opt for the more serious charge.

v. Theft

The statistics and court records suggest that the overwhelming majority of thefts reported and prosecuted were opportunist and petty. However, where employee theft was involved, the magistracy tended to take a much firmer stance as regards sentencing. In addition, the value of the property stolen would impact upon the outcome of the trial.

vi. Bastardy

This offence centred on the neglect of a father to maintain a child, thereby burdening the already overstretched Parish Relief. The offence was considered to be socially-divisive, hence its inclusion as a 'Principal Offence'.

Miscellaneous Offences

i. Reputed Thieves

The Habitual Criminals Act (1869) and the Prevention of Crime Act (1871) gave the police considerable supervisory powers over those who had been convicted of more than one offence and could therefore be considered 'reputed' or 'habitual' criminals. Police could arrest such persons on suspicion, and it was incumbent on the accused to show that they did not intend mischief when apprehended.

ii. Miscellaneous Offences

Included in this over-arching category were such offences as brothel-keeping, desertion from the army and navy, nuisances against local acts, common misdemeanours, forgery and embezzlement.

iii. Wilful Damage

This offence involved deliberate and malicious damage caused to commercial property and public buildings, quite often associated with drunk and disorderly behaviour and less often, public order offences such as unlawful assembly and riot. Physical damage to property in the form of arson was included in this offence.

iv. Prostitution

Statistically, prostitution does not appear to have featured prominently in the local crime figures. However, there is evidence that Bolton's magistracy did take firm action with those 'unfortunate women' when they were arrested. Particularly during the second half of the nineteenth century, there seems to have been some determination to clean up on 'street crime' of which prostitution was one type.

v. Assault and Police Obstruction

Assault towards authority, namely the police, was a common feature in the crime statistics throughout the nineteenth century. Included in this offence was the act of rescuing or attempting to rescue persons legally apprehended by the police. The 'assault' element of the offence also included common assault and 'maiming or cutting'.

vi. Vagrancy

This offence included deserting families, begging and collecting alms, obstructing the highway, wandering about and lodging in out-houses and indecent exposure. The arrest figures for the offence suggest that there was a specific aim of deterring would-be tramps and vagrants from entering the town by such action. The figures for discharges support this 'shock and deterrent' policy.

vii. Receiving and Possession

This particular offence was often committed by petty thieves who turned 'front men' to whom stolen goods would be passed. These in turn, would end up with pawnbrokers or second-hand shopkeepers. The police were always concerned about pawnbrokers acting as receivers. Some unquestionably did, though many probably simply preferred not to ask questions and others must have received stolen goods unknowingly.

Old clothes dealers were suspect in the same way that pawnbrokers were. So too were the owners of chandler's shops who might receive and resell whatever was purloined from ships by dockers. There were scrap-metal dealers who asked no questions about small quantities offered to them for sale. There were also grocers who received, repackaged and resold goods. It is, of course, most unlikely that many of these necessarily made significant profits from such activities, or that many of them could, in any significant way, be considered as 'professional' criminals.

viii. Gambling

Included in this offence would be illegal betting and gaming on licensed premises and street gambling, both regular features of nineteenth-century town life.

ix. Assault and Wounding

This serious offence involved wounding or causing grievous bodily harm - with or without intent. Convictions for the offence usually carried a significant prison sentence. The offence was incorporated into ss. 18 and 20 of the Offences Against the Person Act (1861). Quite often, the offence was committed where violent clashes between rival factions occurred, such as between English and Irish workers in the industrial towns of northern England, especially during the middle years of the nineteenth century.

x. Rape and Attempted Rape

Sexual assaults were always notoriously under-reported. During the nineteenth century there appears to have been a reluctance among women and girls to report sexual offences because of embarrassment and stigma within the strict legal mores of the Victorian era. In addition, many working-class women were probably discouraged by the reluctance of male officials to take such charges seriously, especially when a man from a higher social group was involved. If a trial did take place, the woman's 'character' was as much at issue as the man's acts. In some cases involving middle-class women, they were able to conceal sexual assaults under prosecutions for breach of promise.

xi. Manslaughter

This offence involved the unlawful killing of a person 'without the intention to kill or inflict grievous bodily harm'. It can be 'voluntary', for example where death results from an assault made under 'provocation', or 'involuntary' where death occurs accidentally from an unlawful act.

Murder and Attempted Murder

While people were concerned about homicide throughout the nineteenth century, the offence never appears to have been statistically prominent. A closer examination of Victorian homicides reveals that while the fears may have been centred on being murdered by a burglar, in most homicides both assailant and victim were known to each other or were often related. It is generally acknowledged that since homicide is regarded as a most serious offence, it is probably more often reported than any other offence. The statistics for homicide are therefore probably closer to the 'real' level of the offence, than is the case with other crimes. However, the extent to which homicide levels can be regarded as a guide to the overall level of inter-personal violence is somewhat speculative.

Statistical Analysis

Table 3 (i)
Principal Offences: Bolton 1850-1880

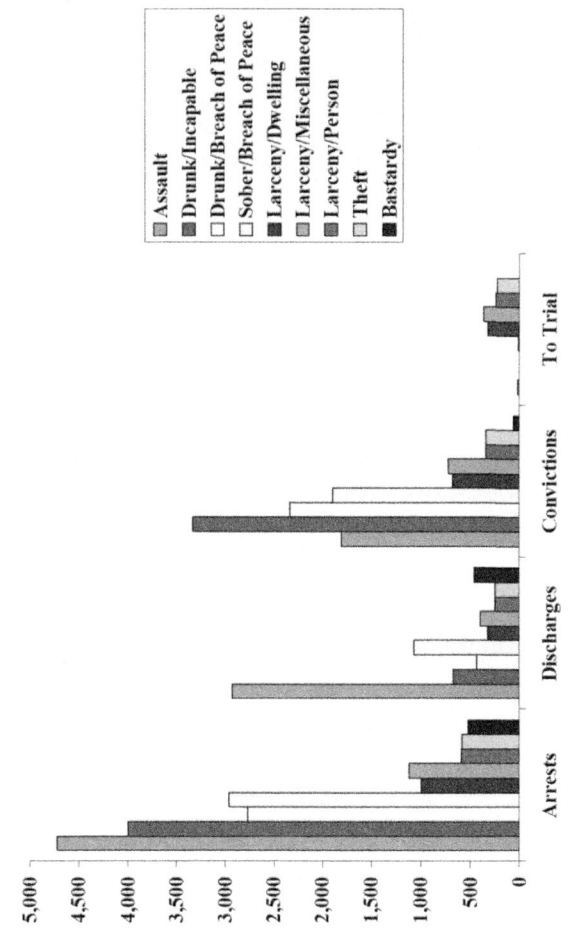

Legend:
- Assault
- Drunk/Incapable
- Drunk/Breach of Peace
- Sober/Breach of Peace
- Larceny/Dwelling
- Larceny/Miscellaneous
- Larceny/Person
- Theft
- Bastardy

Categories: Arrests, Discharges, Convictions, To Trial

Source: *Chief Constable's Reports to the Bolton Watch Committee, 1849-1880 (Bolton Archives Department).*

David Holding

Table 3 (ii)
Miscellaneous Offences: Bolton 1850-1880

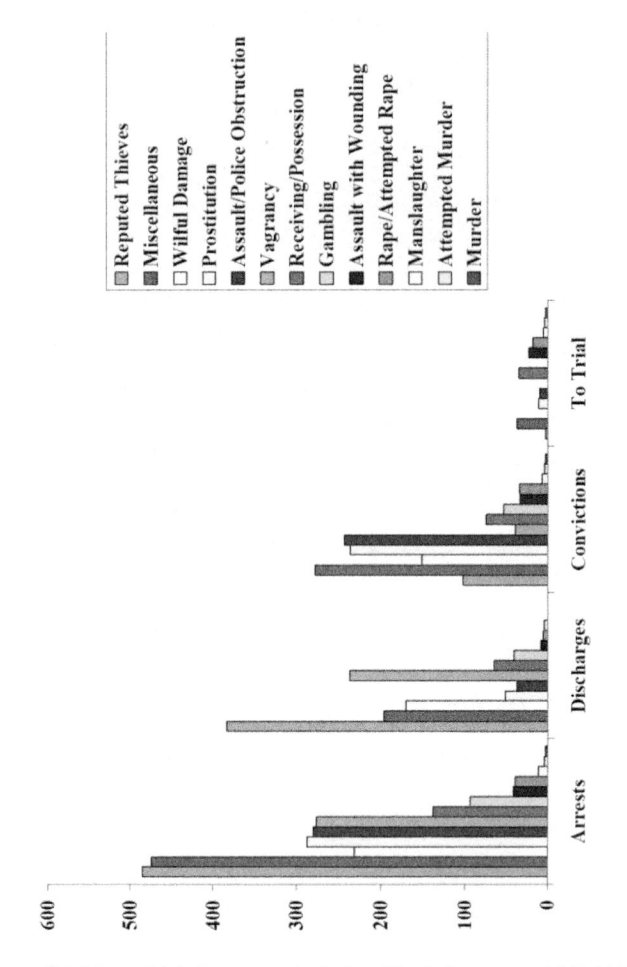

Source: Chief Constable's Reports to the Bolton Watch Committee, 1849-1880 (Bolton Archives Department).

**Table 3 (iv)
Arrests**

Principal Offences: Bolton 1850-1880

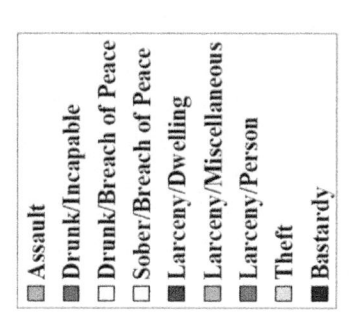

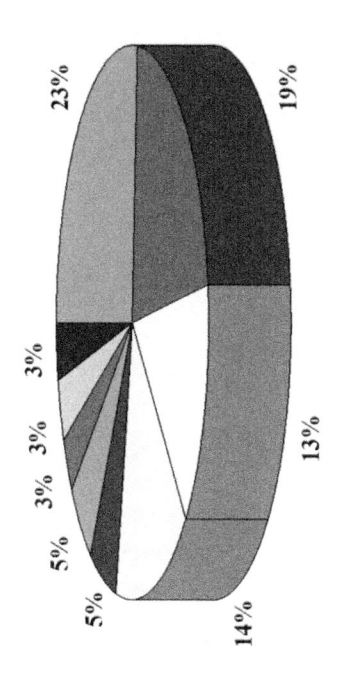

- Assault
- Drunk/Incapable
- Drunk/Breach of Peace
- Sober/Breach of Peace
- Larceny/Dwelling
- Larceny/Miscellaneous
- Larceny/Person
- Theft
- Bastardy

23%, 19%, 13%, 14%, 5%, 5%, 3%, 3%, 3%

David Holding

Miscellaneous Offences: Bolton 1850-1880.

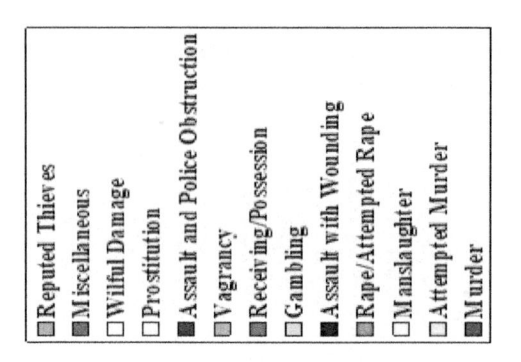

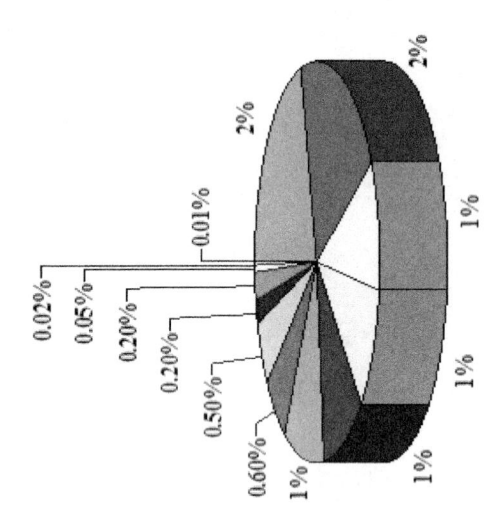

Legend:
- Reputed Thieves
- Miscellaneous
- Wilful Damage
- Prostitution
- Assault and Police Obstruction
- Vagrancy
- Receiving/Possession
- Gambling
- Assault with Wounding
- Rape/Attempted Rape
- Manslaughter
- Attempted Murder
- Murder

Values shown on chart: 2%, 2%, 1%, 1%, 1%, 1%, 0.60%, 0.50%, 0.20%, 0.20%, 0.05%, 0.02%, 0.01%

N.B. Arrests for specific offences shown as a percentage of the total arrests for the period.

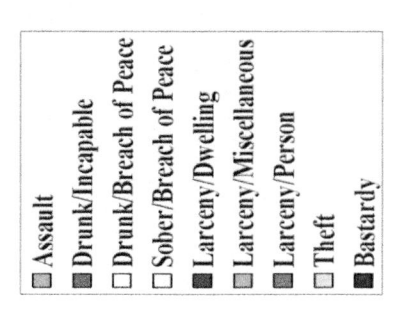

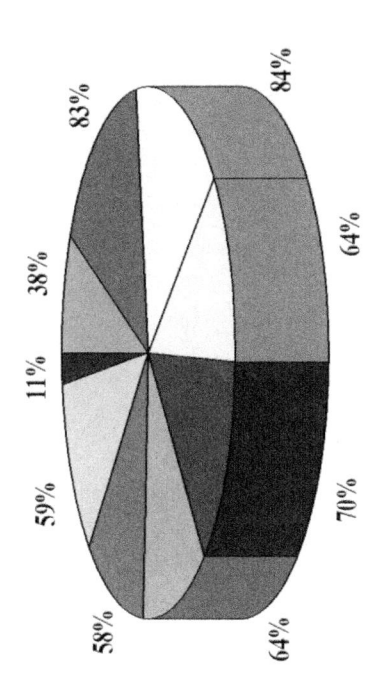

Table 3 (v)
Convictions

Principal Offences: Bolton 1850-1880

- Assault
- Drunk/Incapable
- Drunk/Breach of Peace
- Sober/Breach of Peace
- Larceny/Dwelling
- Larceny/Miscellaneous
- Larceny/Person
- Theft
- Bastardy

84%
83%
64%
38%
11%
70%
59%
58%
64%

David Holding

Table 3 (vi)
Convictions

Miscellaneous Offences: Bolton 1850-1880

Legend (offences):
- Reputed Thieves
- Miscellaneous
- Wilful Damage
- Prostitution
- Assault and Police Obstruction
- Vagrancy
- Receiving/Possession
- Gambling
- Assault with Wounding
- Rape/Attempted rape
- Manslaughter
- Attempted Murder
- Murder

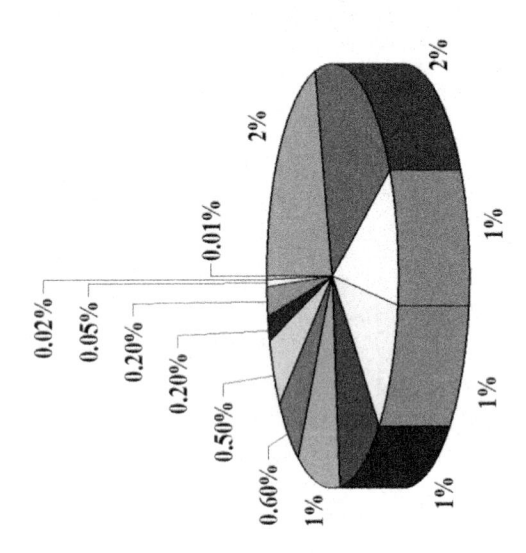

Values shown on chart: 2%, 2%, 1%, 1%, 1%, 1%, 0.60%, 0.50%, 0.20%, 0.20%, 0.05%, 0.02%, 0.01%

N.B. Conviction figures shown are as a percentage of arrests for the offence over the period.

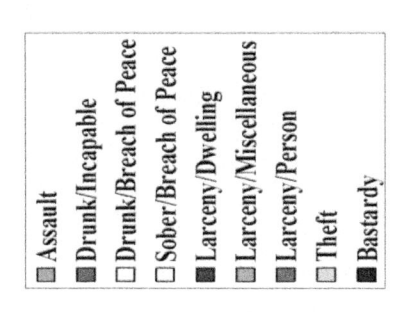

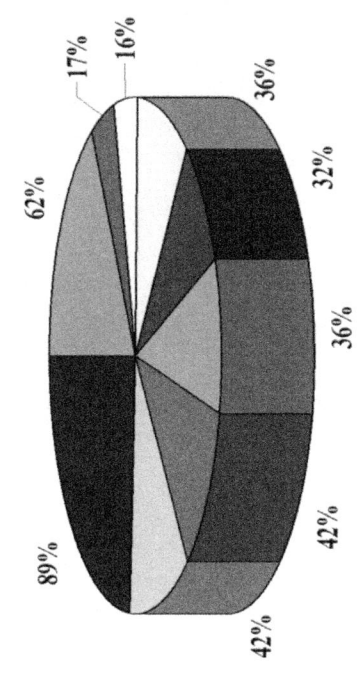

Table 3 (vii)

Discharges

Principal Offences: Bolton 1850-1880

David Holding

**Table 3 (viii)
Discharges**

Miscellaneous Offences: Bolton 1850-1880.

N.B. Discharges shown as a percentage of arrests for the specific offence over the period.

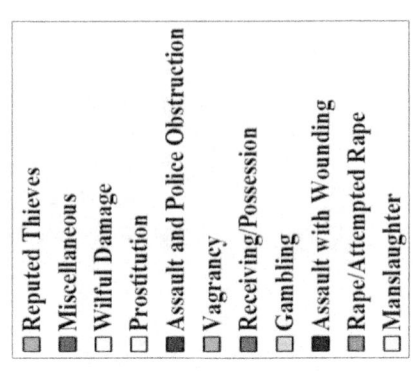

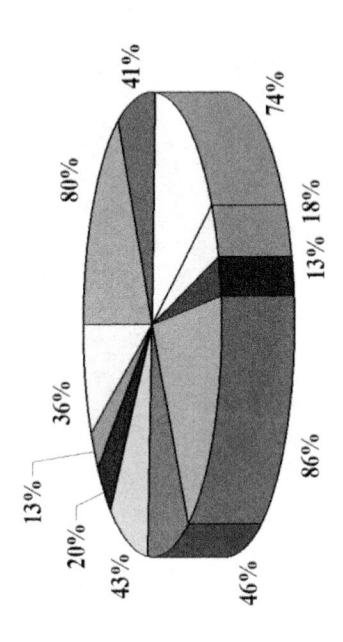

- Reputed Thieves
- Miscellaneous
- Wilful Damage
- Prostitution
- Assault and Police Obstruction
- Vagrancy
- Receiving/Possession
- Gambling
- Assault with Wounding
- Rape/Attempted Rape
- Manslaughter

41%, 74%, 80%, 18%, 13%, 36%, 86%, 13%, 20%, 43%, 46%

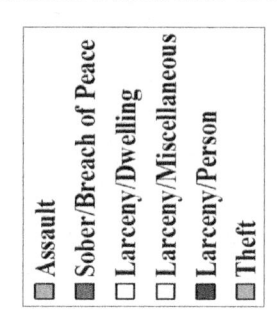

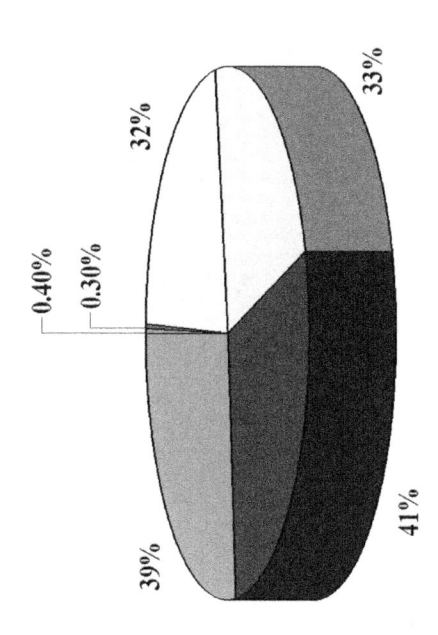

The Dark Figure: Crime in Victorian Bolton

Table 3 (ix)

To Trial on Indictment

Principal Offences: Bolton 1850-1880

- Assault
- Sober/Breach of Peace
- Larceny/Dwelling
- Larceny/Miscellaneous
- Larceny/Person
- Theft

0.40%
0.30%
32%
33%
39%
41%

Table 3 (x)
Trial on Indictment

Miscellaneous Offences: Bolton 1850-1880

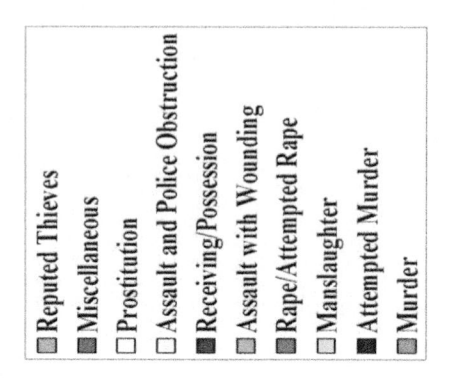

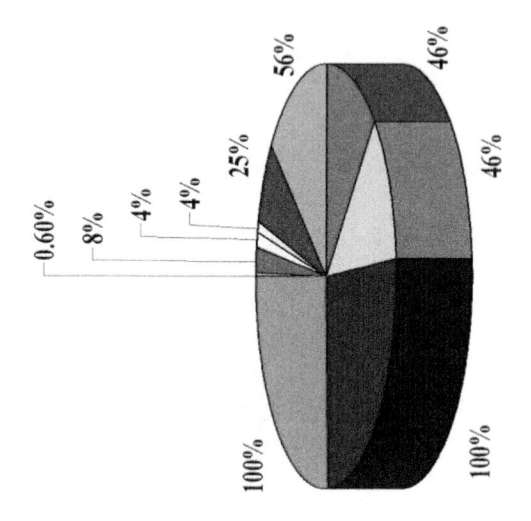

N.B. Trials on Indictment are shown as a percentage of arrests for the specific offence over the period.

Principal Offences. - Table 3 (xi)

Arrests

In terms of absolute numbers, there were four offences which were predominant: Assault (4,720), Drunk and Incapable (3,996), Drunk with Breach of the Peace (2,765) and Sober with Breach of the Peace (2,960).

Discharges

There were two main offences with the highest numbers of discharge, Assault (2,923) and Sober with Breach of the Peace (1,121).

Convictions

It is not altogether surprising that the four main categories of offence having the highest conviction rate should be the same as those for arrests; Assault (1,797), Drunk and Incapable (3,327), Drunk with Breach of the Peace (2,330) and Sober with Breach of the Peace (1,889).

To Trial

Those committed for trial were in the main, on charges of Larceny in various forms and of Theft (1,148), with a small number committed on charges of Assault (19) and Sober with Breach of the Peace (8).

Miscellaneous Offences - Table 3 (xii)

Arrests

In strict numerical terms, there were five offences that were statistically significant. These were Reputed Thieves (485), Miscellaneous Offences (474), Prostitution (287), Assault and Police Obstruction (280) and Vagrancy (276).

Discharges

The highest number of discharges to arrests were for four offences; Reputed Thieves (383), Vagrancy (237), Miscellaneous Offences (196) and Wilful Damage (150).

Convictions

In terms of convictions, four classes of offences were significant; Miscellaneous Offences (278), Assault and Police Obstruction (243), Prostitution (236) and Wilful Damage (151).

To Trial

Those committed to trial on indictment were in the main from Miscellaneous Offences (37), Receiving and Possession (35) and Assault with Wounding (23).

Arrests as Percentages -Table 3 (xiii)

Principal Offences

There were four main offences which accounted for 69% of the total arrests for the period 1849-1880. They were; Assault (23%), Drunk and Incapable (19%), Sober and Breach of the Peace (14%), and Drunk and Breach of the Peace (13%).

Miscellaneous Offences

There were six offences which were statistically significant and accounted for a total of 8% of the total arrests for the period. These were; Reputed Thieves (2%), Miscellaneous Offences (2%), Wilful Damage (1%), and Vagrancy (1%).

Convictions as Percentages of Arrests -Table 3 (xiv)

Principal Offences

There was a total of eight offences with the highest percentage of convictions to arrests over the period which accounted for 65% of the total convictions. These were; Drunk with Breach of Peace (84%), Drunk and Incapable (83%), Larceny in Dwelling (70%), Sober with Breach of the Peace (64%), Larceny Miscellaneous (64%), Theft (59%), Larceny of the Person (58%) and Assault (38%).

Miscellaneous Offences

There were six offences which when combined produce a total of 8% of convictions to arrests. These were; Reputed Thieves (2%), Miscellaneous Offences (2%), Wilful Damage (1%), Prostitution (1%), Assault and Police Obstruction (1%), and Vagrancy (1%).

Discharges as a Percentage of Arrests - Table 3 (xv)

Principal Offences

There were four categories of offences with the highest percentage of discharges to arrests over the period. These were identified as; Bastardy (89%), Assault (62%), Larceny of the Person (42%) and Theft (42%).

Miscellaneous Offences

There were five categories of offences of statistical significance: Reputed Thieves (80%), Vagrancy (86%), Wilful Damage (74%), Receiving and Possession (46%), and Gaming (43%). These accounted for 66% of discharges to arrests.

Committed to Trial as a Percentage of Arrests - Table 3 (xvi)

Principal Offences

There were four offences which are of statistical importance in terms of the number committed to Trial on indictment. These are identified as Larceny of the Person (41%), Theft (39%), Larceny Miscellaneous (33%) and Larceny in dwelling (32%). These offences accounted for 36% of committals.

Miscellaneous Offences

There were six offences which when combined, accounted for 62% of the total committed to trial. These were Murder (100%), Attempted Murder (100%), Assault with Wounding (56%), Rape and Attempted Rape (46%), Manslaughter (46%), and Receiving and Possession (25%). The remaining 2% of offences were made up of Prostitution (0.08%), Reputed Thieves (0.02%), Miscellaneous Offences (0.29%) and Assault and Police Obstruction (0.09%).

Extracts from the Bolton Borough Police: Chief Constable's Reports to the Bolton Watch Committee – 1849-1880.

'There has been a decrease in the numbers apprehended, much fewer than during any year since the establishment of the present police force. The Beer Act has been found to be the means of checking drunkenness very considerably. There has been a decrease in the numbers of apprehensions for drunkenness.

The general character of crime does not differ materially from that in previous years. There has been a considerable decline in some of the more serious offences, e.g. breaking into premises, robbery from the person with violence and larceny.

Out of forty-one reports against publicans, only five escaped penalties and out of fifty-six reports against beer-sellers, only four charges were not proven.'

October, 1849

'There has been a general decrease in apprehensions throughout the year, with a considerable diminution in the class of the more serious offences. This has resulted in a great measure from the continued improved state of trade, the satisfactory condition of the working class and a general and unexampled prosperity.

The number arrested was 2,767 of which 1,474 were summarily convicted and 106 sent for trial. There has been a favourable decrease in offences against property committed with violence. There have been only 883 apprehensions for drunkenness. As regards the conduct of public-houses and beer-houses, I regret to state that the complaints against the latter increased by twelve this year.'

October, 1852

'The total apprehensions were 2,600 with an increase in offences against the person. The principal increase is in common assaults and assaults on constables.

No improvement has taken place as regards the conduct of public-houses and beer-houses. Most drunkenness has, I believe, been prevented during the last two years by the inducements held out by the railway company with respect to cheap trips. These means of recreation have been to a great extent, adopted and appreciated by the operatives and their families.'

October, 1853

'The total number of apprehensions was 2,006, of which 1,020 were summarily convicted and 121 sent for trial. The decrease in drunkenness has been attributed principally to the great drain of idle and dissolute persons who have been carried off by the recruits which have been going on for the army and navy; those persons being taken from the adult population, and particularly from among the characters who usually indulge in intoxicating drinks.

Another reason might be assigned; the high price of provisions and limited employment which the operatives have been subjected to during the last winter and spring of this year. The Returns show a decrease in the number of that floating population which pass more or less daily through the town. I would recommend for the suppression of vagrants, the every one of them be committed when the case is proved against them.

There is another class of individual which require a most vigilant watchfulness on the part of the police, namely the recently discharged ticket-of-leave men. That they be not allowed to congregate in numbers; that they be removed off the streets at night in good time; that they keep from associating with former acquaintances in vice and crime, and that they be encouraged, if possible, to work and be industrious. All these are matters of vital importance and too much attention cannot be paid to them.

I have directed my attention to the juvenile class of offenders who live generally by petty theft and vagrancy. Most of these children, who are orphans, left without any proper protection, and others are abandoned by their parents. I am glad to find they are considerably on the decrease, owing principally to the benefit some of them received in the Ragged School established in this town. I am happy to say this has been a means of inducing many to lay aside their bad habits.

I am happy to inform you that the Borough is in a very healthy, quiet and orderly state. Industry is moderately plentiful in the Borough, although there are some branches which have suffered much from 'stinted' employment. Wages are good, but on the other hand food is exceedingly dear.'

October, 1855

'There was a decrease in the numbers apprehended from 2,190 in 1857 to 1,391 this year. There was a larger number of unemployed operatives, and many only partially employed. The number in full employment is 18,471, a decrease of 1,319 on the previous year.'

October, 1858

'The total number arrested was 2,237, consisting of 1,591 males and 646 females. There was a predominance of male over female offenders.'

October, 1860

'The total arrests were 1,939, a decrease on the previous year. It was to be expected that there would be a considerable augmentation in the number of juvenile offenders, owing to the scarcity of employment and the dearness of food which necessarily offer powerful inducements for dishonesty. The state of employment is gradually improving so far as factory operatives are concerned.'

October, 1862

'The total arrests were 2,061, a decrease of 5% on 1864. A very large number of tramps have passed through the town during the last twelve months; 81,590 or 7,666 above the population of Bolton at present [73,924]. There are very few unemployed and all the large establishments in the Borough are in full work.'

October, 1865

'The number arrested was 2,596, made up of 1,867 males and 729 females. There has been a considerable decrease in the number of arrests of unfortunate women.'

October, 1868

'There has been a considerable decrease in the number apprehended for vagrancy; 297 in 1869 and 217 this last year.'

October, 1870

'Those convicted of felony totalled 295; of these 12 adults could read and write well, 101 could read and write imperfectly; 112 could neither read nor write; 36 juveniles were able to read and write imperfectly' and 34 had no education whatsoever. With reference to publicans and beer-sellers; their establishments have been well-conducted and during the past year they are desirous of keeping within the pale of the law.'

October, 1873

'The total number reported for indictable offences was 205. Of these, 173 were arrested and 127 committed for Trial. There has been an increase in the value of property stolen from £646 last year to £846 this year. There has been a decrease in robberies from shops but an increase in the value of property stolen. There were 994 arrested for the offence of being Drunk and Disorderly of which 77% were male and 23% female. There was an increase in the number of 'disorderly prostitutes' totalling 134; 80 were arrested for Assault on Police. There are now in the Borough 41 male and 7 female convicts, 4 of whom hold licenses and the licenses of the remaining 37 have expired. During the year, 2 males and 1 female have had their licences revoked for misconduct.'

October, 1877

'The number of persons arrested for burglary, together with house and shop breaking was 20; an increase on the previous year. A decrease in 'disorderly prostitutes' to 80 compared to 106 in 1878. Assaults on police have increased from 60 to 89, whilst there was a decrease in the numbers apprehended for breach of the peace, from 866 in 1878 to 611 this last year. The number of offenders prosecuted for wilful damage was 44, of which 24 were discharged or settled out of court; 4 were imprisoned and 16 were fined.'

October, 1879

'The total arrests this last year was 2,836, of which 724 were discharged and 2,112 convicted and disposed of. 504 were committed to prison, 3 to Reformatory Schools and 17 to Industrial Schools. 342 provided sureties to keep the peace. There was a decrease in drunk and disorderly offences, down to 471.'

October, 1880

While the extracts from the Chief Constable's Annual Reports provide only a superficial overview of criminality in Bolton, they are nonetheless useful as an historical source. They draw attention to the fluctuations in criminal activity and also provide an insight into the police perception of crime. It appears that there were significant variations over time in arrest rates and the types of offence being committed.

The Dark Figure: Crime in Victorian Bolton

Table 3 (xvii)
Number of Morning Drunkards Arrested – Bolton 1860

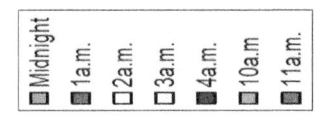

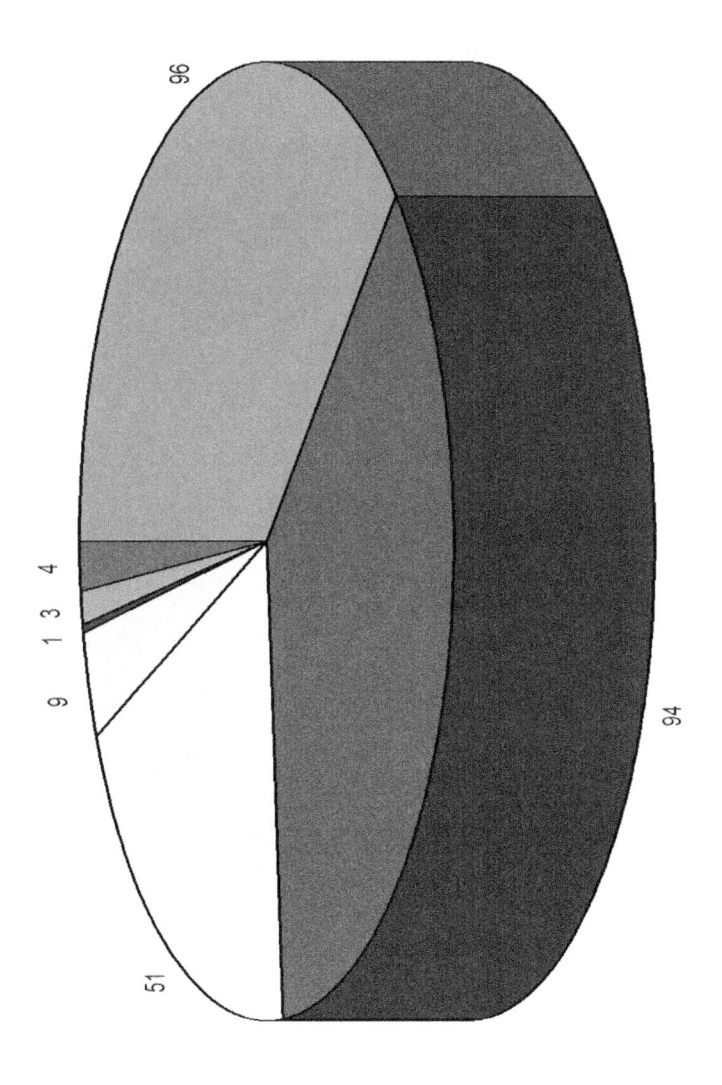

Table 3 (xviii)

Number of Afternoon Drunkards Arrested- Bolton 1860
Source: Bolton Borough Police Return – 1860 (Bolton Archives Department).

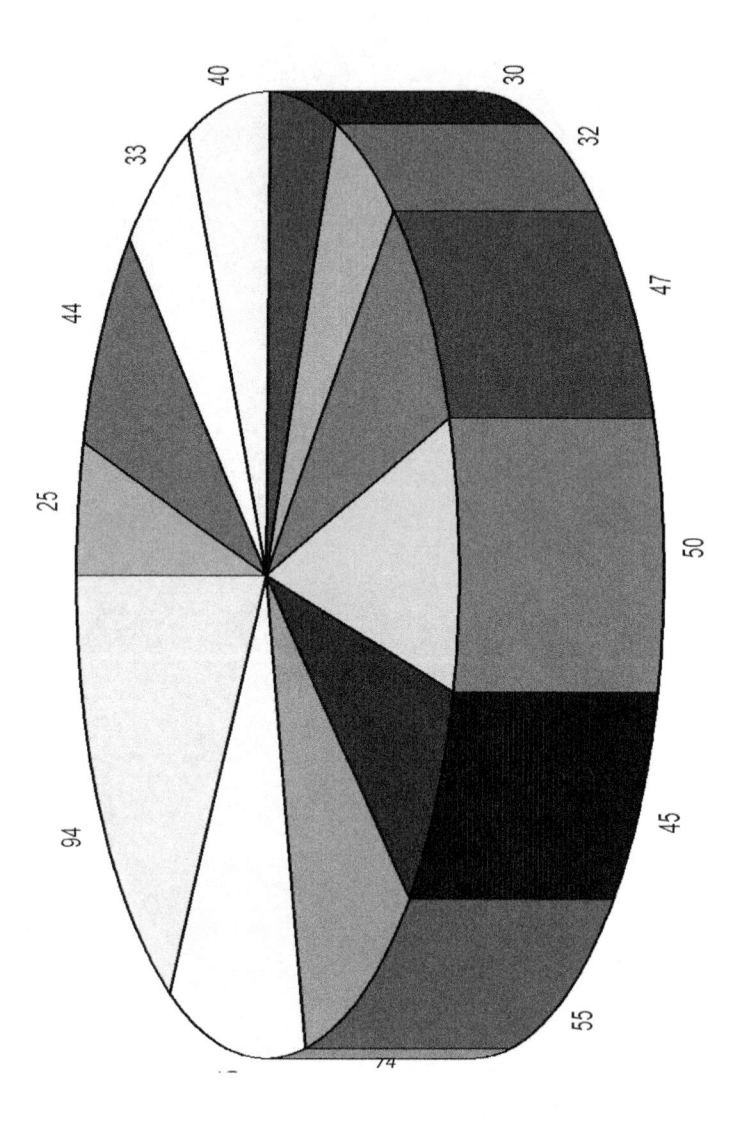

Most participants in the discussion of crime in the nineteenth century agree that drink was a prominent factor. Many of the public houses and beer-houses in Bolton were patronised by the working-classes throughout the day. The breakdown of times of arrest for drink-related offences on the previous table shows a clear pattern. The majority of offences occurred between 11 p.m. and 2.00 a.m., a pattern familiar today, despite the more flexible opening hours for licensed premises. It is of relevance to note that the prescribed hours for drinking during the period amounted to a staggering 16 hours per day on weekdays and 6½ on Sundays. The hours of closing for licensed premises were; weekdays 10.00 p.m. to 6.00 a.m. and Sunday 3.00 p.m. to 6.00 p.m. and 10.00 p.m. to 6.00 a.m.

In effect, on weekdays public-houses were open for the consumption of alcohol for 16 hours and 13 hours on Sundays. Pubs served as an unobtrusive agent in the criminal life of Bolton and most other towns, and this was fuelled by their great number, the majority being concentrated in the poorer districts of towns. By today's standard, the availability of drinking establishments and the number of persons engaged in the drinks trade was extraordinary.

The periods from 1861 to 1864 show increases in drink-related convictions and those for assault, whilst during the periods of relative prosperity e.g. 1865-67, there was a decrease in convictions for assault, but little overall change in drink-related convictions. Thus, the figures for Bolton reveal a pattern that is different to that suggested by the work of Gatrell and Hadden. They carried out an analysis by correlating the figures of convictions for assault and drunkenness with the national business cycle, to show slight increases in these offences during years of relative prosperity. This, they maintain, suggests that higher wages and high employment led to a greater consumption of alcohol which, in turn, contributed to more violent crime.[48]

There are two possible conclusions to be drawn from these findings for Bolton. Either assaults were not as closely-linked to drink as Gatrell and Hadden suggest, or Bolton's working-class saw drink as an integral component of their culture. However, this does not necessarily negate the generally accepted view of the relationship between drink and violence. There is no doubt that in times of hardship Bolton's working-

---

[48] V.A.C. Gatrell, and T.B. Hadden, *'Nineteenth –Century Crime Statistics'*, pp. 269-71 & 370-71.

class sought some consolation in drink and the resultant assaults were a further manifestation of the despair and apathy they experienced throughout the nineteenth century.

There is no doubt that drink-related offences, assault and breaches of the peace were common features of criminality in Bolton throughout the nineteenth century. There was no significant rise in the more serious offences. It is significant to note that the police acknowledge the impact that economic factors could have had upon certain criminal offences, in particular, petty theft. This was particularly evident during periods of high unemployment when food was expensive and 'necessity became a very powerful inducement for dishonesty'.

References are made to increases in juvenile delinquency and police support for the reformatory system as a means of reducing crime. There appear to have been periods when the police in Bolton revealed their optimism as regards the state of the town: e.g. 'the town is in a very healthy, quiet and orderly state' (1855). One wonders to which section of society these sentiments were addressed; these views are hardly reflective of the majority of the working-class of Bolton.

There is little doubt that the Chief Constable's comments would be used as a springboard for future policy decisions by members of the Watch Committee, many of whom were magistrates themselves. There is no direct evidence that the comments had a direct influence on sentencing policy but neither would they be completely ignored. It is of relevance to note that towards the end of the nineteenth century, references are made to an increase in the value of property stolen. This does suggest that thieves were specifically targeting premises and perhaps becoming more sophisticated in their activity, or shopkeepers and private residents were becoming somewhat complacent.

Prostitution does not appear to have been a major feature in the crime statistics although there are references to fluctuations in terms of both arrest and conviction rates. The specific reference to ticket-of-leave men suggests that the majority did serve out their probationary periods satisfactorily, although they were still targeted by the police. This is further evidence of the importance the police attached to 'labelling' offenders and the 'categorising of criminal groups' so evident in the later nineteenth century. The majority of those convicted were disposed of summarily usually by a fine or surety to keep the peace.

The statistical data available on crime in Bolton is limited to the years from 1849 to 1880, and this makes generalisations regarding criminal activity in the town somewhat speculative. The Chief Constable's Reports provide only a partial record of criminality over the period. The high discharge rates for some offences make it difficult to assess whether this was a result of police inexperience in presenting cases or an unwillingness to convict on the part of the magistrate in summary cases, or the jury in trials.

Theft and assault figures were affected by legislation, particularly when indictable offences were shunted into summary jurisdiction categories. For example, a succession of Acts were passed in the mid-nineteenth century; the Juvenile Offenders Act (1847), a second Juvenile Offenders Act (1850) and the Criminal Justice Act (1855). The consequent fall in committals on criminal indictments was erroneously taken as a real fall in crime. However, when the statistics of convictions at both quarter sessions and under summary legislation are considered, there appears a marked increase in crime.

Taking the various forms of raw crime statistics over the period, a pattern begins to emerge - a gradual decline in theft and violence, but with housebreaking and burglary remaining constant. Within this overall pattern there are marked annual fluctuations, as well as peaks and troughs extending slightly longer than a year. These statistics suggests that the most common crime (between 50 and 75 per cent) throughout the period was small-scale theft, the great majority of offenders being male.

Assaults on police formed a regular percentage of assaults and declined at a slower rate than common assault. Placing the figures for assault and drunkenness alongside the business cycle, slight increases during the years of prosperity suggest that high wages and high employment led to a greater consumption of alcohol which, in turn, contributed to more violent crimes. However, for the last quarter of the nineteenth century, the overall trend for both violent crime and drunkenness is markedly downwards.

Analysis of the statistics and the content of indictments taken together with a variety of other evidence suggest two things. Firstly, enlistment in time of war removed those persons from the community who most commonly were indicted for property offences in times of peace, namely young men in their late teens and early twenties. Such young men seem to have been particularly vulnerable to the temptation of criminal activity for a variety of reasons. Secondly, it was often only when these young men were removed from the community that the impact of dearth became really apparent in the figures for theft. In the years of dearth, which coincided with war, figures for indictments for property crime can be seen to go up, and married men and women for whom wheat prices were of vital importance to the family budget, became more evident as the accused.

Yet there is a problem which may undermine this war/theft relationship, namely the number of young men who were apprehended in wartime but who before any indictment was preferred against them, were encouraged or pressurised to enlist in the forces. Exact figures are difficult to determine, yet there appear to have been very large numbers recruited in this way, numbers quite possibly sufficient to account for the drop in indictments during wartime.

Acquittals and discharges are far more frequent in lower courts and may reflect a policy adopted by the magistrates to deal with certain categories of offences leniently. However, circuit judges at Quarter Sessions, with no local ties, were more likely to convict. Local magistrates responded in different ways to different offences. Women in general were treated more leniently than men, whilst men were far more likely to be found guilty.

Overall, the larceny statistics for the second half of the nineteenth century show some correlation between the peaks of offences known to the police and the years of high unemployment and need. Criminality in the form of thefts committed by men from the poorer sections of the working class was transitory behaviour, possibly fostered by economic hardship, probably encouraged by opportunity. While there seems to be an interplay between criminal statistics and periodic fears of crime and disorder, it is also probable that the collection and publication of national crime statistics led to the perception of crime as a national and impersonal problem. During the eighteenth century, when there were no such statistics, crime was essentially a personal problem for victims and accused.

Statistics made crime national and made the criminal a national 'bogeyman'. Crime could now be shown to be offences perpetrated on a large scale against respectable people by a group which, by being measured statistically, could be defined collectively as criminals or as the 'criminal' class. However, most thefts and cases of violence cannot be attributed to 'professional' criminals, nor is it helpful to think of these offences as being committed by a group which could in any meaningful sense, be described as a 'class'.

The statistics of committals and indictments which form the basis of the criminal statistics, are obviously some way from any measurement of actual crime. They are the end product of a variety of filters and require at the very least a victim prepared to prosecute - or someone prepared to report an offence, and an individual who has been accused and apprehended. Equally important is the fact that individual prosecutions were also the product of a social, economic and political context which changed from decade to decade and even from year to year. Thus, in some years the context may have provoked a ferocious response to a particular offence, in others, the response could have been far more muted.

Chapter Four:

Punishment or Reformation?

Prosecutions and Sentencing Trends

The English legal system provides for any private citizen to initiate a prosecution. Well over 80% of prosecutions in the nineteenth century were conducted by the victims of crime or, less frequently, by private individuals acting on the victim's behalf. Victims of a criminal offence had a variety of choices; they could let the matter drop if they regarded it as too insignificant for a criminal prosecution. Employers could, and often did, simply dismiss workmen. Many victims were satisfied with the return of their stolen property and with the scare that they gave the accused by the fact of reporting it to the police.

In a strictly forensic sense, assaults were different from thefts in that they were not necessarily felonious. Alternative settlements to prosecution continued to be sought and found in cases of assault throughout the nineteenth century. Moreover, it would seem that many working-class prosecutions for assault were part of continued feuds between rival families and groups, the law being employed as one way of the complainant achieving a measure of justice. It was resolved to take the accused to a higher court and the magistrate committed him or her for trial. Bail was very rarely given in larceny cases and committal meant the accused being put into gaol, often for several months before standing trial.

While no nineteenth century legislation had any dramatic impact on the system of prosecution by private individuals, there was a very significant, if gradual, change brought about with the development of the 'new' police.

'The increasing role of the police as prosecutors from the middle of the century has been largely ignored by police historians, and there has been no detailed study, even on a regional basis, of precisely when, how and why the police came to be predominant as prosecutors'.[49]

---

[49] D. Philips, *Crime and Authority in Victorian England*, (Croom Helm, London, 1977), pp.123-4.

Increases in the mobility of the population and the growing size of towns in the nineteenth century did not have to amount to actual urbanisation before the delicate links binding village communities could be strained. The destruction of these links also compelled citizens to turn to different, more formal and institutional modes of punishment. Methods intended to invoke community censure and eventual reconciliation, such as "the three P's" (pillories, processions and public confessions) began to lose meaning.

In the early nineteenth century, there was an emphasis on employing terror into the law, despite the efforts of the criminal law reformers. Later observers were more inclined to classify offences and types of offender and then apply punishment accordingly. Between 1839 and 1870, imprisonment in Britain gradually replaced transportation as the main form of penal servitude. Once it was generally accepted that most offenders should be sent to prison, the crucial arguments centred on the extent to which prison was a place of punishment or reformation. Penal reform began with the abolition of capital statutes urged by Romilly and Mackintosh, and was largely carried out by Peel and Russell. The most serious offences against persons and property, tried at Assizes, were punishable by death, execution being by hanging.

Custodial confinement in some form of institution went back at least to the Middle Ages, and was always available as an option for judges and magistrates. Some petty offenders were sentenced to short periods in prison - the disorderly, the idle and vagrants. With the decline in the use of the death penalty, prisons had more of a central role in the criminal justice system.

Analysis of sentencing trends as indicated in the Bolton Quarter Sessions record for the years from 1840 to 1843 (Table 4 (i)), shows a wide judicial discretion. There is a clear indication that the age of the offenders was less of a consideration than the nature of the offence. However, in the case of female offenders, the prison sentences appear less severe than those for their male counterparts. There is little doubt that many offences were the direct result of the dire necessity experienced during the 'hungry forties'.

There does appear to be some measure of consistency in sentencing as regards offences involving currency, particularly as the very nature of the offences was detrimental to the local economy. This is reflected in the severity of sentence, where 46% of the recorded offences involving currency resulted in transportation ranging from seven years to life. Of the more mundane offences, it is of interest to note that in 1841, two female pickpockets were given one-month imprisonment each. It was very likely that they were related; being either mother or daughter, or were working as part of a team, the younger girl being akin to an 'apprentice'.

Table 4 (i) Bolton Quarter Sessions Record: 1840-1843

1840

Male	19	Theft of Watches.	Nine Months Prison.
Male	15	Theft from Person.	Ten Years Transportation
Female	25	Theft from Person.	One Month Prison.
Male	23	Theft of Fowls.	One Month Prison.
Male	30	Theft from Shop.	Three Months Prison.
Male	16	Theft.	Seven Years Transportation.
Female	22	Theft of Two Sovereigns.	Six Months Prison.
Male	20	Theft of Butter.	Six Months Prison.
Male	15	Theft of Tobacco.	Two Months Prison.
Female	42	Obtaining Groceries.	Three Months Prison.
Male	20	Obtaining Timber.	Six Months Prison.
Male	21	Theft from Person.	Three Months Prison.
Male	19	Theft from Person.	Three Months Prison.
Male	39	Theft of Forty Sovereigns.	Seven Years Transportation.
Male	20	Theft of 55lbs of Beef.	Four Months Prison.
Female	25	Theft of Calico.	Four Months Prison.
Female	36	Theft of Eight Lead Rollers.	Two Months Prison.
Male	28	Theft of Writing Desk.	Acquitted.
Male	32	Theft of Five Pieces of Calico.	Eighteen Months Prison.
Male	18	Theft of Five Packs of 27 shillings in Copper.	Seven Years Transportation.
Male	24	Theft of Ham.	Acquitted.

The Dark Figure: Crime in Victorian Bolton

Male	32	Theft of Two sovereigns.	Acquitted.
Male	22	Theft of Twenty Shillings.	Acquitted.
Male	25	Theft of Twenty Shillings.	Acquitted.
Male	20	Theft of Twenty Shillings.	Acquitted.
Male	23	Theft of Nine Shillings and a Brown hat.	Two Months Prison.
Female	29	Theft of Nine Shillings.	Two Months Prison.
Male	50	Theft of Fifteen Sovereigns.	Acquitted.
Male	30	Theft of Iron Pipe.	Three Months Prison.
Male	19	Theft from Till.	Six Months Prison.
Male	34	Theft of Seven Sovereigns.	Three Months Prison.
Male	20	Theft of One Shirt.	Three Months Prison.
Male	26	Theft of One Chair.	Two Months Prison.
Male	21	Assault on Constable.	Six Months Prison.
Male	20	Suspicious Character with Five Pound Note in his possession.	Ten Years Transportation.
Male	19	Absence from Work as an Apprentice.	Two Months Prison.
Male	26	Neglect of Family.	Six Months Prison.
Male	22	Assault on Police Constable.	Twelve Months Prison.
Male	21	Assault on Market Lookers.	Three Months Prison.
Male	19	Assault on Market Lookers.	Six Months Bail.
Male	42	Bigamy.	Two Months Prison.
Female	32	Theft from Dwelling.	Two Months Prison.

1841

Male	22	Attempted Rape.	Fifteen Years Transportation.
Male	19	Theft of Pie Moulds.	Four Months Prison.
Male	22	Aiding and Assisting in Robbery.	Seven years Transportation.

Male	30	Coining.	Ten Years Transportation.
Male	26	Coining	Ten Years Transportation.
Male	30	Receiving.	Seven Years Transportation.
Male	30	Keeping a Brothel.	Four Months Prison.
Female	30	Keeping a Brothel.	Four Months Prison.
Male	23	Stabbing.	Four Months Prison.
Male	32	Child Abduction.	Twelve Months Prison.
Male	25	Making Base Coin.	Transportation for Life.
Male	42	Making Base Coin	Transportation for Life.
Female	40	Picking Pockets.	One Month Prison.
Female	16	Picking Pockets.	One Month Prison.

1842

Male	43	Possession of Counterfeit Half-Crowns.	Ten Years Transportation.
Male	15	Manslaughter.	Two Months Prison.
Male	14	Manslaughter.	Two Months Prison.
Male	39	Breaking into House and Theft.	Twenty-Two Years Transportation.
Male	30	Rioting and Throwing Stones at Police.	Acquitted.
Male	25	Rioting and Throwing Stones at Police.	Acquitted.
Male	59	Rioting and Plug Drawing.	Two Months Prison.
Male	41	Assault on Child.	Twelve Months Prison.

1843

Male	20	Theft of a Cheese.	Ten Years Prison.

Source: Bolton Borough Police: Sessions Book 1839-1851 (Bolton Archives Dept).

Composition of the Magistracy

From about 1835 onwards, there was a change in the composition of the local magistracy, from a majority of landed gentry to one of industrialists who comprised the principal local employers. This was evident in Bolton in 1853 when the magisterial bench comprised 'Henry and Edmund Ashworth, James Kay, Richard Crompton, Stephen Blair and William Hargreaves, all of whom were local manufacturers'.[50] An analysis of prosecutions under the 1855 Criminal Justice Act in the mid-nineteenth century reveals employee theft to have been the most common offence. It shows that most of the prosecutions were undertaken by small tradesmen and masters rather than by larger firms and employers.[51]

Many of the influences which constrained the Bolton magistracy throughout the eighteenth century; political and religious prejudice, the weight of kinship and friendship networks and pressures from powerful economic groups, still held sway into the early years of the nineteenth century. Whilst a local outlook prevailed on the bench, that outlook narrowed. The Bolton magistracy was drawn very heavily from the local elite of manufacturers. This meant that in cases involving industrial disputes, the ethos of the factory masters prevailed, to the detriment of the worker and small master.

The landed gentry and the 'new industrialists' exercised an important influence over the rate of prosecutions as each group could and did initiate prosecutions. In this way the local gentry could prosecute in their own right and, acting as Justices, could put pressure on the police to enforce laws against publicans, prostitutes and vagrants.[52]

Unlike Lancashire's county government, Bolton's local government was very much in the hands of the new 'bourgeoisie' rather than the old aristocracy, and this enabled successful merchants and industrialists to attain admission to the magisterial bench. The poor employees probably did have the cards stacked against them in summary trials, although there were magistrates who sympathised with them and who were

---

[50] *Whelan and Co, Bolton Directory for 1853*, p. 23.
[51] J. Davis, '*Law Breaking and Law Enforcement: The Creation of a Criminal Class in Mid-Victorian London*', (Boston, 1986), pp. 267-70.
[52] M. De-Lacy '*Prison Reform in Lancashire, 1700-1850*', Chetham Society, 3rd Series, vol 33, (Manchester, 1986), p. 66.

especially critical of those employers who used illegal truck payment.

Partly through public pressure but also no doubt because the ruling class believed the rhetoric of the law's impartiality, magistrates were keen to demonstrate their own lack of bias. According to one study, Wigan magistrates in the early years of the nineteenth century appear to have administered justice with relative impartiality, except in cases of industrial theft when it appears their personal interests took precedence.[53] The Master and Servant Act of 1823 was increasingly used as a strategy in controlling the industrial worker. It is probable that the increasing appointment of professional lawyers as stipendiary magistrates checked the most blatant abuses by employer-justices.

---

[53] Barrett, 'Crime and Punishment', pp. 84-86.

Prisons and Industrial Schools

In the first half of the nineteenth century, prison reform shared the characteristics of other reforms; a gradual shift of initiative from local to central power, the establishment of a central Commission and of a national inspectorate to enforce and superintend government decisions. Research by Michael Ignatieff provides a valuable account of the initial development of the penitentiary and of the motives underlying the reformer's efforts.[54] He adopts the view that the reformers were motivated by concern over the apparent disintegration of the social order. He argues that the economic and social strains of the nineteenth century encouraged those in authority to send more offenders to prison.

The overall character of prisons was determined chiefly by three factors; the nature and number of their inmates, the quality of their staff and the extent of their day-to-day supervision. The size of the prison population was a critical element in the quality of prison life. Prisons can prove to be remarkably resistant to reform imposed from outside. The Lancashire prison system was produced by the interaction of many factors; political events such as the Luddite disturbances, economic problems such as post-war inflation, contemporary preoccupations with such issues as free-speech, representative government and conceptions about reformative punishment.

The size of the prison population directly reflected the rate of prosecutions, but this rate was not an independent variable. It reflected social and economic changes that may have actually increased the number of offences, but it also reflected changes in the willingness of victims to prosecute. In sentencing, no clear distinction was made between the House of Correction and the county gaol; felons and misdemeanants went to both. However, vagrants rarely went to Lancaster Castle whilst debtors never went to the House of Correction. The remaining prisoners went to whichever institution was most convenient at the time.

In Lancashire, the main prisons were at Lancaster, Preston, Kirkdale (Liverpool) and Salford (New Bailey). Evidence from Quarter Sessions Calendars for Bolton suggest that the majority of offenders were sent after trial to Salford

---

[54] M. Ignatieff, *'A Just Measure of Pain: The Penitentiary in the Industrial Revolution, 1750-1850'*, (Macmillan, London, 19878), pp. 124-30.

prison, except in cases of capital charges, when Kirkdale appears to have been the common remand centre.[55] The rising number of petty offenders in penal institutions suggests not only a higher crime rate but also a greater willingness to take formal legal action over complaints previously solved less formally. Enlarged prison capacity made this possible. The Manchester House of Correction was rebuilt in 1774 and again in 1790. Similarly, Preston re-opened on a new site in 1789. In one sense, the prison reformers who built larger prisons may have exacerbated the very problem they wished to solve.

As with policing, development in provincial prisons was limited by cost. Preston Gaol provided the model for the industrial prison with its inmates who were sub-contracted to three local textile firms and allowed a proportion of the monetary value of their work. However, the practice received little support elsewhere, and as a consequence labour in prisons from about 1820 onwards, tended to be increasingly pointless. Activities such as walking the treadmill or picking oakum in the solitude of a cell proliferated. Yet during the 1840s, the inmates of Durham Gaol were producing cloth mats, nets and rags for sale in the nearby market. Salford's New Bailey Prison was first opened in 1790 and used mainly for the detention of minor offenders and those awaiting trial at County Court. It was replaced by Strangeways Prison in 1868 and was finally demolished in 1872. The stark reality of prison conditions in the nineteenth century can be gleaned from details of cell accommodation in Salford's New Bailey Prison.

> 'The dimensions of a cell with single bed, was seven feet three inches long, five feet nine inches wide and eight feet seven and a half inches high. A cell with three beds in it, was twelve feet four inches long, seven feet four inches wide and eight feet four and a half inches high. The walls were one foot nine inches thick and the prison had five hundred and twenty two separate cells.'[56]

If social anxiety lay behind both the increased committal rate and the demand for a more rigorous prison discipline, the two factors to some extent cancelled each other out. The increased reliance on imprisonment to punish petty

---

[55] *Quarter Sessions Calendar, 1853-1870,* (Bolton Archives Department).
[56] T. Frankland, *@Salford's Prison: An Account of the New Bailey Prison',* (Warrington, 1983), pp. 8-10.

offenders eventually led to extremely short average terms of confinement. These short terms made nonsense of the reformers' ambitious plans. During the 1850s, a band of devoted reformers including Mary Carpenter and Matthew Davenport-Hill, spoke in favour of reformatories and industrial schools. In 1853, a Select Committee on Crime and Destitute Children recommended a degree of state assistance for Reformatory Schools. The Youthful Offender Act of 1854 provided for persons under sixteen years to be sent to such school.

The need to separate young offenders - and thus prevent their total corruption by hardened recidivists - had been urged for generations. As early as 1818, magistrates in Birmingham were sentencing juveniles to short terms in a local reformatory founded by private subscription.[57] Under the Newcastle Act of 1861, industrial schools were to be of two kinds; uncertified and certified, the only distinction being that under the provisions of the 1854 Act, the certified industrial schools received and detained children or pauper children, for whose maintenance and education the Guardians could contract. The attendance of other children at both certified and uncertified schools was voluntary. The object of these schools was to reclaim children who, from the circumstances of their homes or from neglect, were in imminent danger of becoming criminal. This object was accomplished by separating them from their connections and giving them instruction in some honest means of earning a living.

The reformers often attributed a perceived decline in juvenile crime during the second half of the nineteenth century, to the reformatory and industrial schools. It is, of course, unlikely that such a decline can be put down to one single factor - gradual economic and social improvement was also a significant factor. It is clear that there was no common sentencing policy with reference to juveniles, and the number of places available in these schools varied between localities. The majority of convicted juveniles continued to be sent to ordinary gaols, and whilst some prisons did offer opportunities to their inmates, few seriously questioned the necessity of education and reforming juvenile offenders.

The Bolton Chronicle for 1850 carried an article outlining the suggestion for the provision of an Industrial School within the Borough.

---

[57] Margery, *The Invention of Juvenile Delinquency*, pp. 11-27.

Juvenile Mendicity in Bolton

'Under this title, Mr. P. R. Arrowsmith has published a letter addressed to the Mayor, suggesting the establishment of a 'Ragged School' in the Borough, with a view to the relief of the town from the danger and cost of permitting the children of the very poor, to be bred in our streets to the practice of begging and pilfering'. [58]

The matter was again brought to the attention of Bolton Council in 1853:

Council Proceedings – Reformatory Schools

'Mr. P. R. Arrowsmith begged the permission of the Mayor and the Council, to offer some remarks on a subject not named in the notice paper. He said there was now before Parliament, a Bill for the purpose of providing, that which magistrates had, in the exercise of their duty, felt to be one of the greatest desiderations in society, namely the establishment of Reformatory Schools. He believed that great proportion of the time of every magistrate was taken up in trying offences of children, and instead of sending them to prison to learn the business of crime, this Bill had the very humane and laudable object of providing schools for the reformation of such criminals. He moved that the Council petition Parliament for the approval of such a Bill, through the Town's member. The proposition was put and carried with no objections'.[59]

By the end of 1853, Mr Arrowsmith had himself been elected Mayor of Bolton and called a public meeting to discuss further the setting up of an Industrial School in the town:

---

[58] *Bolton Chronicle, 13 July 1853*, p. 4.
[59] *Bolton Chronicle, 30 July 1853*, p.3.

Bolton Industrial Ragged School

'At an influential preliminary meeting of the inhabitants of the Borough of Bolton and its neighbourhood, favourable to the establishment of an Industrial Ragged School, the following resolutions were unanimously passed: That in the opinion of this meeting, a great amount of juvenile destitution, ignorance and crime has long existed in this Borough, for which no adequate remedy has yet been provided. It appears to this meeting, that a large number of the present aggregate of crime might be so prevented, and numbers of miserable human beings converted into virtuous, honest and industrious citizens, if due care were taken to rescue these neglected and criminal children. The Ragged Schools existing in this county have produced beneficial effects on the children of the most destitute classes of society; it is therefore desirable that a similar institution should be established in this Borough'.[60]

A public subscription list was opened, and a Committee formed to oversee the Fund. The response was such that the total of £2,535 was received within six months, enabling the Committee to buy suitable premises in Commission Street. In April 1854, the Committee interviewed seventeen applicants for the posts of Master and Matron of the school. By June 1854, the Bolton Industrial School was opened.

By 1857 there were 378 children in attendance at the school and the premises proving to be too small - it became necessary to move to new premises at Lostock Junction in 1870. The following statistics show the number of children admitted to the school in 1869, their ages and background, the state of literacy on admission and the number who found employment after leaving the school.

---

[60] *Bolton Chronicle, 31 December* 1853, p.7.

Table 4 (ii).
Bolton Industrial School: 1869.

Age on Admission:

Under 6	6 to 8	8 to 10	10 to 11	Over 12	Total
0	12	25	120	30	187 (64%)

Parentage:

Illegitimate.	Orphans.	Parents Dead.	Deserted.	Criminal
45 (24%)	30 (16%)	38 (20%)	38 (20%)	36 (20%)

State of Instruction on Admission:
Neither Read nor Write   70 (37%)
Read and Write Imperfectly   90 (48%)
Read and Write Well   27 (14%)

Classification on Admission:
Begging: 10
Found Wandering: 65 (35%)
Frequenting the company of reputed thieves: 9
Residing in Brothels: 12
Charged with offence punishable by Imprisonment: 22 (12%)
Uncontrollable by Parents: 10
Refractory Pauper: 6
Non-compliance with School Attendance Order: 26 (14%)
Habitually Wandering in the company of Rogues: 12
Misbehaving at Day Industrial School: 15

Situation on Release from School:
To employment or service found by the School: 40 (43%)
Returned to Friends of Decent Character: 27 (29%)
Returned to Friends of Questionable Character: 7
Sent to Sea: 2
Enlisted: 17
Discharged due to Illness: 1
Absconders: 0

Source: Alice Holt, 'Bolton Certified Industrial School', (Bolton, 1978), p. 26.

These figures show that the highest number of children admitted were from the 'found wandering' class, some sixty-five or 35% of the total. This was followed by children who did not attend school regularly at 14% of the total. Finally, there were those who had committed a crime at 12% of the total. These figures further indicate that the majority of boys found regular employment after their discharge from the school, and none to the time the figures were compiled had been convicted of a crime. Support in Bolton was widespread, and the Industrial School was seen as a very real means of reclaiming children from criminal opportunity:

> 'The Industrial School at Lostock admirably carries out the purposes for which it was designed. The lads, snatched from a life of sin, are taught useful trades such as joinery, tailoring, shoe-making, cotton spinning and agriculture. The effect upon juveniles of this salutary tuition, is patent to the most casual observer of the lads when introduced to the school, and a few months afterwards. Bright and happy faces are visible everywhere.'[61]

Corporal punishment was used to correct bad behaviour as was loss of privileges. Some boys were sent to the school for truancy. In 1863, the Committee places the school under the provisions of the Industrial Schools Act of 1857, which meant that it was eligible for Training Grants for the maintenance of children detained by magistrates' order. This also meant that admission to the school was no longer limited to the Bolton Borough; the area of admission was widened to include surrounding districts.

One interesting fact emerges from a study of the Register of Admission, which shows that over a third of the children admitted during the years 1856 and 1857 were from Roman Catholic families. This was an inevitable result of the Famine years in Ireland.[62] After a period at the school, boys could be discharged or licensed out to work in the local community, the equivalent of the present-day Community Service Orders:

> 'The cotton mills at Lostock Junction were always supplied throughout the year with a considerable number of half-timers'.[63]

---

[61] *Bolton Journal, 3 March 1869*, p.5.
[62] *Bolton Industrial School: Register of Admissions, 1855-1865*, (Bolton Archives Department).
[63] Whittle, *History of Bolton*, p. 290.

It appears from entries in the visitors' book made by inspecting officials of the various School Boards and local Council officials, that the school was fulfilling its obligations, both in the physical case and in preparation for a working life of its inmates. It is possible to ascertain with some accuracy just how strict the discipline was at the Bolton school, and to what extent corporal punishment was used. From official enquiries, it appears that birching was used extensively throughout Industrial Schools. Sport and physical training were encouraged as aids to better health and physique. It is interesting to note how many 'old boys' continued to keep in contact with the school after leaving, and many were willing to visit the school when the opportunity arose. By 1901, the number of admissions was declining, which suggests an increase in parental care of children and also a general rise in the standard of living of the working class.

By way of post-script, any society that does not restrain its citizens to some extent leaves them free to prey on each other - particularly the most vulnerable. However, there comes a point at which restraint imposed in the name of society, can and often does, smother other basic needs and values. An unjustified faith in reformation may have, in turn, led magistrates, judges and reformers to sentence to institutions, many people who should never have gone there in the first place.

Conclusion

The recent growth of academic research and publications (particularly in the history of crime) has been unprecedented in recent years. More general, text book surveys; political, economic and social, rarely address the problem of crime. However, in more recent times, historians have increasingly turned their attention to crime and how former societies understood it and sought to deal with it. The key question posed by this study is - what impact did the enormous economic and social changes of the nineteenth century have on crime in Bolton - as practised by offenders, as defined by legislators and as enforced by state agents?

On one level there is a clear answer to the impact of these changes on criminal behaviour, though it would be nigh impossible to qualify it. Consider increased wealth, more merchandise in shops and warehouses and more movable property in homes - all these provided greater opportunities and greater temptation. The increase in property crime recorded by the admittedly imperfect statistics, especially during the serious economic slumps of the early period of industrialisation does appear significant. However, the assumption that poverty led to theft remains too simple. Economic hardship brought about by slump merely exacerbated the situation and spread temptation further.

Throughout the nineteenth century, theft of various types was the main offence occupying the court's time. Most of these thefts were petty, with only a minority involving large sums of money or items of great monetary value. Only a very few involved violence. It was the quantity rather than the quality of the offence that concerned people most. It could be argued that this has always been the case. However, once the decision had been taken, albeit unconsciously, to concentrate on quantity rather than on what might be termed quality crime, other things naturally followed.

Most offenders brought before the courts for these crimes came from the poorer sections of society. As a consequence, as the discourse on 'class' become more central to the analysis and perceptions of society in the nineteenth century, so criminality tended to be viewed as, essentially, a 'class' problem. Counterfactual history is fraught with danger, yet, if legislators and commentators on crime had concentrated on the few large-scale thefts or embezzlements as their bench mark for crime rather than on the small thefts and incidents of disorder, the overall perception of criminality and of the 'criminal class' would have been very different. This is not to imply that there was a middle-class conspiracy during the nineteenth century when these perceptions persisted.

Concerns about the poor and their 'immoral' or 'disorderly' behaviour go back a long way in history. Of course, it was recognised that men of wealth and social standing did commit criminal offences. From time to time there were public outcries against various forms of 'white-collar' crime and corruption. However, such offenders were rarely perceived as members of a 'criminal class' and then not until the closing years of the nineteenth century, when 'biological' discourse began to rival 'class' discourse in the analysis of crime and criminality.

The illegal or immoral acts of white-collar offenders set a bad example to their social inferiors, but these offenders were the 'rotten apples' within their social class. This was a consoling distinction to which the middle and upper classes clung; that such offenders within their social group were exceptions, the 'criminal class' was to be found located elsewhere. The use of the term 'criminal class' was probably at its most common during the 1860s, but the idea of a criminal class and of professional criminals living, at least partly, by the proceeds of criminal activity, was popular throughout the Victorian period.

The criminal class described by Victorian commentators became largely synonymous with the poorer working-class, particularly those who existed by means of casual labour. However, the very word 'class' implies a large number and a more homogeneous group than existed in reality. The notion of a criminal class was then, and still remains a convenient one for insisting that most crime is something committed on law-abiding citizens by an 'alien' group. However, the more that historians probe this notion, the more it is revealed to be spurious. In the final analysis, it has to be acknowledged that the law defines crime and that legislation can criminalise or decriminalise activities. To this end, criminal behaviour will adapt accordingly.

The reorganisation and rationalisation of the criminal law, the changes in punishment and the creation of new organs of containment and control, are all linked with the changing economic and social order. Whatever the statisticians have argued about improvements in life expectancy, the numerous tables published during the middle years of the nineteenth century reveal a significant difference between the life expectancy of the working-class and that of their social superiors. The physiological differences between working-class, particularly the poorer section, and the middle class were certainly a reality.

Crime is rarely something that people experience regularly as victims, and their perceptions of crime therefore depend largely on what they are told about it. It is clear that 'crime waves' and 'moral panics' could be accelerated during the nineteenth century by the press eager to boost sales or crusade for changes in the penal system. The publication of national crime statistics, together with faith in the new 'science' of statistics, and the repetition of notions like the concept of the 'dangerous classes' possibly served to foster the perception of a longer-term crime wave in the first half of the nineteenth century. As concerns about crime were heightened, so arguably, more crime was reported and prosecuted.

The increase in statistics was not just the result of more crime. By the same token, the general stability of the Victorian social order in the second half of the nineteenth century, the faith in progress and the belief that the police and courts were improving and winning the war against crime, may have contributed to a decline in the reporting and prosecution of the more petty offences. The main argument put forward for establishing the 'new' police was that they could prevent crime. From the moment they took to the streets, most of the new police were also deployed to enforce new concepts of order on the working class. There was heightened concern about order in the early nineteenth century which ultimately led to the use of the police in enforcing particular conceptions of behaviour and respectability. However, enforcing order was generally easier than preventing or detecting crime, and by emphasising their 'order' role, the new police could demonstrate an efficiency and effectiveness which was nowhere near as apparent in their crime-prevention role.

A statistical increase in indictments for petty theft during the years of dearth may reflect a genuine increase in theft brought about by necessity. The establishment of the new police invariably produced local increases in the numbers of individuals committed for public order offences - being drunk and disorderly or drunk and incapable, obstructing the highway and vagrancy. These offences were essentially 'public' and arrests relatively easy. Directives to individual police forces to clamp down on any such offences could produce a sudden peak in local crime statistics.

Environmental issues such as population expansion, health, housing and employment, all impacted on the types and extent of crime in Bolton during the Victorian period. Most contemporaries considered that the evils of the working-class were self-inflicted. However, such short-sighted generalisations overlooked the more obvious facts. Early death deprived families of essential income, whilst periods of unemployment created not only boredom and apathy, but also led to extreme poverty.

The real problem was that many analysts of nineteenth century crime ignored the seasonal and uncertain nature of much employment. The gruelling aspects of working-class existence contributed to a marked difference between the classes. It is against the background of these social and economic differences that the nature and extent of crime in Victorian Bolton must be considered.

Selected Bibliography

This bibliography is organised in the following manner:

1. **Primary Sources**
1a. Newspapers and Journals.
1b. Manuscript Collections.
1c. Parliamentary Papers.
1d. Books and Articles by Contemporaries.

2. **Secondary Sources**
2a. Unpublished Theses and Dissertations.
2b. Books and Articles.

Primary Sources

1a. Newspapers and Journals
Bolton Chronicle: 1850-1870.
Bolton Free Press: 1838-1848.
Bolton Journal: 1869.

1b. Manuscript Collections (Bolton Archives Department)
Bolton Borough Police Records.
Charge Book: 1840-41.
Court Minute Books: 1829-65.
Daily Memoranda of Incidents: July to September, 1839.
Quarter Sessions Record: 1839-60.
Returns of the Chief Constable: 1853-70.
Record Book of Crime and Stolen Property: 1860.
Watch Committee Reports: 1838-47.

Miscellaneous Manuscripts
Great Bolton Overseers of the Poor: Accounts for 1837.
Register of Admissions: Bolton Industrial School: 1856-7.
Register of Births: Fletcher Street Workhouse, 1839.
Letter from Rev. J.S. Slade, Vicar of Bolton to the Trustees of Great Bolton, October 1840.

1c. British Parliamentary Papers
Select Committee Report on Criminal Committals and Convictions, H.C. (vi).
Select Committee Report on Public Houses. H.C. (xxxvii).

Select Committee Report on the Police of the Metropolis, H.C. (vi).
Select Committee Report on Drunkenness, H.C. (xxii). 1836.
First Report of the Inquiry into the Conditions of the Poorer Classes in Ireland. Report on the State of the Irish Poor in Great Britain. Appendix G. H.C. (xxxiv).
Select Committee Report on Transportation, H.C. (xxii).
Royal Commission on Constabulary Forces H.C. (xix).
Census of Great Britain: Population Tables, vol ii (Lxxxv).
Select Committee Report on the Police, H.C. (xxxiv).
Census of England and Wales, vol ii (Lvi), (C.873).
Poor Law Report, H.C. (xxxvii).

1d. Books and Articles by Contemporaries
Ashworth, H., 'Statistics of the Depression of Trade in Bolton', Journal of the London Statistical Society, (1842).
Baines, E., History of the County Palatine and Duchy of Lancaster, 2 vols, (London, 1868).
Ballard, J., Report to the Registrar-General on the Sanitary Conditions of Bolton, (Bolton, 1872).
Barratt & Son, Commercial Directory of Bolton, 1890.
Bent, J., Criminal Life: Reminiscences of Forty-Two Years as a Police Officer, (Manchester, 1891).
Black, J., 'A Medico-Topographical, Geological and Statistical Sketch of Bolton and its Neighbourhood', Transactions of the Provincial Medical and Surgical Association, vol v, (1837).
Brimelow, W., A Political and Parliamentary History of Bolton, 2 vols, (Bolton, 1882).
Caminada, J., Twenty-Five Years of Detective Life, (Manchester, 1895), reprint, 1982.
Clarke, G.T., Report to the General Board of Health on the Borough of Bolton, (London, 1849).
Clegg, J., A Chronological History of Bolton, (Bolton, 1878).
Clegg, J., Annals of Bolton, (Bolton, 1888).
Entwistle, J., Report on the Sanitary Conditions of the Borough of Bolton, (Bolton, 1848).
Greenwood, J., The Seven Curses of London, (London, 1891), reprint, Blackwell, Oxford, 1981.
Morrison, W.D., Crime and its Causes, (London, 1891).
Pigot and Dean, Directory of Bolton, (Bolton, 1821-2).
Pigot and Sons, Bolton Directory, (Bolton,1836).
Scholes, J.C., History of Bolton with Memorials of the Old Parish Church. (Bolton, 1892).

Slater & Co., Bolton Directory, (Bolton, 1843).
Taylor, J., Autobiography of a Lancashire Lawyer, (Bolton, 1883).
Whellan & Co., Bolton Directory, (Bolton, 1853).
Whittle, P.A., History of Bolton-le-Moors, (Bolton, 1857).

Secondary Sources

2a. Unpublished Theses and Dissertations
Barrett, P.C., 'Crime and Punishment in a Lancashire industrial town: Law and Social Change in the Borough of Wigan, 1800-50' (M.Phil. Thesis, Liverpool Polytechnic, 1980).
Dale, P.N., 'A Study of the Growth of Churches in Bolton during the Industrial Revolution', (Ph.D. Thesis, University of North Wales, 1984).
Davis, J., 'Law Breaking and Law Enforcement: The Creation of a Criminal Class in Mid-Victorian London', (Ph.D. Thesis, Boston College, 1984).
Else, W.J., 'Industrialisation and the Religious Life of Bolton, 1832-1914', (M.Phil Thesis, University of Salford, 1992).
Holding, D., 'A Profile of Criminality in Victorian Bolton', (MA Thesis, Manchester Metropolitan University, 1996).
Holding, D., 'Conflict and Assimilation: Irish Communities in Bolton and Preston, 1840-1914', (Ph.D. Thesis, Manchester Metropolitan University, 2002.)
Kirk, N., ' Class and Fragmentation: Some Aspects of Working-Class Life in South-East Lancashire and North-East Cheshire, 1850-1870', (Ph.D. Thesis, University of Pittsburgh, 1974).
Macnab, K., 'Aspects of the History of Crime in England and Wales between 1805 and 1860', (Ph.D. Thesis, University of Sussex, 1965).
Motte-De, C.M., 'The Dark Side of Town: Crime in Manchester and Salford, 1815-75', (Ph.D. Thesis, University of Kansas, 1977).
Taylor, P.F., 'Popular Politics and Labour-Capital Relations in Bolton, 1825-50', (Ph.D. Thesis, University of Lancaster,1991).

2b. Books and Articles
Anderson, M., Family Structure in Nineteenth Century Lancashire, (Cambridge U.P. 1971).

Bailey, P., Leisure and Class in Victorian England, (Lancaster U.P. 1978).
Bailey, V., Policing and Punishment in Nineteenth Century Britain, (Croom Helm, London, 1981).
Beatie, J., "The Criminality of Women in Eighteenth Century England", Journal of Social History, 8 (1975).
Best, G., Mid-Victorian Britain, 1851-75, (RKP, London, 1971).
Boyson, R., The Ashworth Cotton Enterprise: The Rise and Fall of a Family Firm, (Oxford U.P. 1970).
Chesney, K., The Victorian Underworld, (Penguin, Harmondsworth, 1970).
Cooper, D., The Lessons of the Scaffold, (Allan Lane, London, 1974).
Crowther, M., The Workhouse System, 1834-1919: The History of an English Social Institution, (Methuen, London, 1983).
Cullen, M., The Statistical Movement in Early Victorian Britain: The Foundations of Empirical Social Research, (Harvester, Brighton, 1975).
Emsley, C., Policing and its Context, 1750-1900, (Macmillan, London, 1983).
Emsley, C., Crime and Society in England, 1750-1900, (Longman, London, 1987).
Englander, D., Landlord and Tenant in Urban Britain, (Oxford U.P. 1983).
Finnegan, F., Poverty and Prostitution: A Study of Victorian Prostitutes in York, (Cambridge U.P., 1979).
Fitzpatrick, D., 'A Curious Tramping People: The Irish in Britain, 1801-1870', in Vaughan, W.E. (ed) A New History of Ireland, 5 vols, (Oxford U.P. 1989).
Frankland, T., Salford Prison: An Account of the New Bailey Prison in 1836), (Warrington, 1983).
Gatrell, V.A.C., 'The decline of theft and violence in Victorian and Edwardian England', in Gatrell, Lenman and Parker (eds), Crime and the Law: The Social History of Crime in Western Europe since 1500, (Europa, London, 1980).
Gatrell, V.A.C. & Hadden, T.B., 'Crime statistics and their interpretation', in Wrigley, E.A. (ed,), Nineteenth century society: Essays in the use of quantitative methods for the study of social data, (Cambridge, U.P., 1972).
Ginswick, H., Labour and the Poor in England and Wales: 1849-51, 8 vols, (Cass, London, 1983).
Goslin, R.J., Duty Bound: A History of the Bolton Borough Police, 1839-1969, (Bolton, 1970).

Hanson, H., The Canal Boatmen, 1760-1914, (Manchester University Press, 1975).
Harrison, B., Drink and the Victorians: The Temperance Question in England, 1815-1872, (London, 1971).
Hawkings, D.T., Criminal Ancestors, (London, 1992).
Holt, A., Bolton and Lancaster Certified Industrial School: A Brief History, (Bolton, 1972).
Ignatieff, M., A Just Measure of Pain: The Penitentiary in the Industrial Revolution, 1750-1850, (Macmillan, London, 1978).
Jones, D., Crime, Protest, Community and Police in Nineteenth Century Britain, (RKP, London, 1982).
Jones, D. 'The New Police, Crime and People in England and Wales, 1829-88', Transactions of the Royal Historical Society, 5th series, vol 33, (1983).
Kirk, N., The Growth of Working Class Reformism in Mid-Victorian England, (Beckenham, 1985).
Klare, H.J., The Changing Concept of Crime and its Treatment, (Oxford U.P, 1966).
Lacy-de, M., 'Prison Reform in Lancashire, 1700-1850', Chetham Society, 3rd series, vol 33, (Manchester, 1986).
Lacy-de, M., 'Grinding Men Good: Lancashire Prisons at Mid-Century', in Bailey,V. (ed), Policing and Protest in Nineteenth Century Britain, (Croom Helm, London, 1981).
Matthews, D., The Trade Cycle, (Cambridge, U.P., 1959).
Margary, S., 'The Invention of Juvenile Delinquency in Early Nineteenth Century England', Labour History, No 34, (1978).
Mather, F.C., Public Order in the Age of the Chartists, (Manchester, U.P., 1959).
Midwinter, E.C., Social Administration in Lancashire, 1830-1860, (Manchester U.P, 1967).
Midwinter, E.C., Law and Order in Early Victorian Lancashire, (York,1968).
Pelling, H., Popular Politics and Society in Late-Victorian England (London, 1968).
Philips, D., Crime and Authority in Victorian England, (Croom Helm, London,1977).
Poole, R., Popular Leisure and the Music Hall in Nineteenth Century Bolton, (Lancaster U.P, 1982).
Priestley, P., Victorian Prison Lives, 1830-1914: British Prison Biography, (Methuen, London, 1985).
Read, D., 'Chartism in Manchester', in Briggs, A. (ed), Chartists Studies, (London, 1965).

Rose, A.G., 'Trucking Magistrates of Lancashire in 1842', Transactions of the Lancashire and Cheshire Antiquarian Society, vol 83, (1985).
Rule, G., 'Outside the Law Studies in Crime and Order, 1650-1850', Exeter Papers in Economic History, No 15, (University of Exeter, 1982).
Steedman, C., Policing the Victorian Community: The Formation of English Provincial Police Forces, 1856-1880, (RKP, London, 1984).
Sellin, T., 'The Significance of the Records of Crime', Law Quarterly Review, Lxv, (1951).
Storch, R.D., 'The Plague of Blue Locusts: Police Reform and Popular Resistance in Northern England, 1840-57' in International Review of Social History, xx (1975).
Stevenson, J., Popular Disturbances in England, 1700-1870 (London, 1979).
Swift, R., 'Urban Policing in Early Victorian England, 1835-56, A Reappraisal', History, vol 73, No 238, (June, 1988).
Tebbutt, M., Making Ends Meet: Pawnbroking and Working-Class Credit, (Leicester U.P, 1983).
Tobias, J.J., Crime and Industrial Society in the Nineteenth Century, (Penguin, Harmondsworth, 1972).
Tobias, J.J., Nineteenth Century Crime: Prevention and Punishment, (Newton Abbot, 1972).
Walton, J.K, Lancashire: A Social History, 1558-1939, (Manchester U.P, 1987).

Printed in Great Britain
by Amazon